DIRECTIONS
a guide to **Key Documents** in Health and Social Care
1986-2002

DIRECTIONS
a guide to **Key Documents** in Health and Social Care 1986-2002

3rd edition
edited by: Lyn Crecy

Contributors:

Anne Brown
Lyn Crecy
Anne Henderson
Susan Martin
Nicola Tricker

University of Plymouth

London: TSO

TSO

Published by TSO (The Stationery Office) and available from:

Online
www.tso.co.uk/bookshop

Mail, Telephone, Fax & E-mail
TSO
PO Box 29, Norwich, NR3 1GN
Telephone orders/General enquiries: 0870 600 5522
Fax orders: 0870 600 5533
E-mail: book.orders@tso.co.uk
Textphone: 0870 240 3701

TSO Shops
123 Kingsway, London, WC2B 6PQ
020 7242 6393 Fax 020 7242 6394
68-69 Bull Street, Birmingham B4 6AD
0121 236 9696 Fax 0121 236 9699
9-21 Princess Street, Manchester M60 8AS
0161 834 7201 Fax 0161 833 0634
16 Arthur Street, Belfast BT1 4GD
028 9023 8451 Fax 028 9023 5401
18-19 High Street, Cardiff CF10 1PT
029 2039 5548 Fax 029 2038 4347
71 Lothian Road, Edinburgh EH3 9AZ
0870 606 5566 Fax 0870 606 5588

TSO Accredited Agents
(see Yellow Pages)

and through good booksellers

© University of Plymouth 2000

This is the third revised edition of
A guide to key documents in health care for nurses, midwives and health visitors 1986-1997
originally published in 1997

Third edition 2002

ISBN 0 11 702961 0

Printed in the United Kingdom for The Stationery Office
ID112793 C20 09/02 19585 772383

Contents

	Introduction	7
	Chronological Index	9
1	**General**	17
2	**Primary and Community Care**	33
3	**Public Health**	49
4	**Quality, Accountability and Patient Rights**	55
5	**Education**	71
6	**Older People**	81
7	**Children**	91
8	**Midwifery**	109
9	**Mental Health**	115
10	**Learning Disabilities**	127
	Applying for Jobs: Suggested Reading	133
	Organisations	135
	Websites	139
	Alphabetical Index	141

Introduction

This is the third edition of a guide to more than 200 key reports and legislation published on health and social care in the last sixteen years.

It offers:

- a guide for students embarking on health, medical and social care careers
- a reminder of the main landmarks for those going to interview
- a background of information for individuals new to health and social care

The new edition has been expanded to include two new chapters: **Public Health** and **Quality, Accountability and Patient Rights**. All other sections have been revised and updated. Documents should be available to borrow or request from your local academic or medical library; some are available in full text on the internet. *Directions* is divided into 10 chapters arranged as follows:

1. General
2. Primary and Community Care
3. Public Health
4. Quality, Accountability & Patient Rights
5. Education
6. Older People
7. Children
8. Midwifery
9. Mental Health
10. Learning Disabilities

These headings are very broad and not mutually exclusive. The documents are arranged in chronological order and each is referenced with an abstract. Where there has been discussion in the press, this has been added as references in **Further Reading**. Many of the documents stem one from another and so we created a **chronological index** at the front, with page references.

For those who will be using *Directions* to prepare for job interviews, **Applying for Jobs** contains a reading list on writing c.v.s, interview technique and career development. *Directions* also lists the main **national organisations** that influence health and social care, gives their contact details and a brief statement of purpose. There are short lists of **abbreviations** and **websites**, and finally an **alphabetical index** at the back.

The range of documents is not exhaustive: (at times, documents are specific to England only, for example) but it includes those that have been 'most asked for' in our experience; where appropriate, chapters include a list of **supplementary reading**. As new policies and reports emerge, *Directions* will be updated. In the meantime, any ideas or amendments are welcome.

The abstracts are the authors' own, resulting from reading the original documents. They are meant to offer a broad outline of policy and thinking in health and social care but in no way do they replace the originals. If you need to read *The NHS plan (2000)* you must read it, the authors accept no responsibility for any misunderstandings or decisions made on the basis of the text of this book.

For their help in the production of this guide, we should like to thank our colleagues, in the IHS and AIS at the University of Plymouth as well as the publisher Roger Tomlinson and Richard Middleton at the Editorial Offices of The Stationery Office.

Lyn Crecy, Learning Resources Centre,
Somerset College of Arts and Technology,
Wellington Road, TAUNTON TA1 5AX

May 2002

Chronological Index

date	title	page
1983	Mental Health Act 1983: chapter 20.	115
1986	Making a reality of community care.	33
1986	Neighbourhood nursing: a focus for care. (Cumberlege report)	33
1986	Project 2000: a new preparation for practice.	71
1987	Promoting better health.	34
1988	Community care: agenda for action. (Griffiths report)	34
1989	Caring for people: community care in the next decade and beyond.	35
1989	Children Act 1989: chapter 41.	91
1989	The consumer's view: elderly people and community health services.	81
1989	The NAWCH quality review: setting standards for children in health care.	91
1989	A strategy for nursing.	17
1989	Working for patients.	17
1989	Working for patients working paper 10: education and training.	71
1990	National Health Service and Community Care Act 1990: chapter 19.	17
1990	The report of the post registration education and practice project.	71
1990	Safeguarding standards.	55
1990	Setting standards for adolescents in hospital.	92
1991	Caring for people: community care in the next decade and beyond - mental handicap nursing. (Cullen report)	127
1991	Just for the day: children admitted to hospital for day treatment.	92
1991	Nursing in the community. (Roy report)	36
1991	The patient's charter.	55
1991	Report of the proposals for the future of community education and practice.	36
1991	Welfare of children and young people in hospital.	92
1992	Child protection: guidance for senior nurses, health visitors and midwives.	92
1992	The Children Act 1989: what every nurse, health visitor and midwife needs to know.	93
1992	The health of the nation: a strategy for health in England.	49
1992	Homeward bound: a new course for community health.	37
1992	Leaving hospital: elderly people and their discharge to community care.	81

date	title	page
1992	Maternity services. (Winterton report)	109
1992	Nurses, Midwives and Health Visitors Act 1992: chapter 16.	18
1992	Nursing education: implementation of Project 2000 in England.	72
1992	Through a glass darkly: community care and elderly people.	81
1993	Bridging the gaps: an exploratory study of the interfaces between primary and specialist care for children within the health services.	93
1993	Changing childbirth. (Cumberledge report)	109
1993	Children first: a study of hospital services.	93
1993	The named nurse, midwife and health visitor.	19
1993	New world, new opportunities: report of a task group in primary health care.	37
1993	Report of the taskforce on the strategy for research in nursing midwifery and health visiting. (Webb report)	18
1993	The rights of the child: a guide to the U.N. convention.	93
1993	Targeting practice: the contribution of nurses, midwives and health visitors.	49
1993	A vision for the future.	19
1994	The Allitt inquiry: independent inquiry relating to the deaths and injuries on the children's ward at Grantham and Kesteven General. (Clothier report)	94
1994	Better off in the community? The care of people who are seriously mentally ill.	116
1994	The care of sick children: a review of the guidelines in the wake of the Allitt inquiry.	95
1994	The challenges for nursing and midwifery in the 21st century. (Heathrow debate)	20
1994	Finding a place: a review of mental health services for adults.	116
1994	The future of professional practice: the Council's standards for education and practice following registration.	72
1994	Half a century of promises: the failure to realise community care for older people.	82
1994	The health of the nation: a handbook on child and adolescent mental health.	94
1994	The health of the nation key area handbook: mental illness. 2nd ed.	115
1994	The interface between junior doctors and nurses. (Calman report)	19
1994	Into the 90s: a discussion document on the future of the health visiting practice.	37
1994	The patients's charter: maternity services.	110
1994	Public health in England: roles and responsibilities of the Department of Health and the National Health Service.	50
1994	Seen but not heard: co-ordinating community child health and social services for children in need.	95
1994	Setting standards for children undergoing surgery.	94

date	title	page
1994	Working in partnership: a collaborative approach to care. (Butterworth report)	115
1995	Carers (Recognition and Services) Act 1995: chapter 12.	38
1995	Continuing the commitment: the report of the learning disability nursing project.	127
1995	Developments in midwifery education and practice: a progress report.	110
1995	Disability Discrimination Act 1995: chapter 50.	128
1995	The doctor's tale: the work of hospital doctors in England and Wales.	20
1995	The health of the nation: a strategy for people with learning disabilities.	127
1995	Learning disability: meeting needs through targeting skills.	127
1995	Making it happen: public health - the contribution, role and development of nurses, midwives and health visitors.	50
1995	Mental Health (Patients in the Community) Act 1995: chapter 52.	116
1995	Midwifery educational resource pack: the challenge of Changing childbirth.	111
1995	The patient's charter and you.	55
1996	Building bridges: a guide to inter-agency working for the care and protection of severely mentally ill people.	117
1996	Building expectations: opportunities and services for people with a learning disability.	129
1996	Child health in the community: a guide to good practice.	96
1996	Choice and opportunity: primary care: the future.	38
1996	Commissioning mental health services.	117
1996	Developing roles of nurses in clinical child health.	96
1996	Health services for children and young people.	96
1996	Learning the lessons: mental health inquiry reports published in England and Wales between 1969 and 1996 and their recommendations for improving practice. 2nd ed.	117
1996	The NHS: a service with ambitions.	21
1996	A new partnership for care in old age.	83
1996	The patient's charter: services for children and young people.	95
1996	Primary care: delivering the future.	39
1996	Primary care: the future.	38
1996	The spectrum of care: local services for people with mental health problems.	116
1996	The standards we expect: what service users and carers want from social services workers.	56
1997	A bridge to the future: nursing standards, education and workforce planning in paediatric intensive care.	101
1997	Child and adolescent mental health services: Health Committee 4th report.	99

date	title	page
1997	The coming of age: improving care services for older people.	83
1997	Developing partnerships in mental health.	118
1997	Emergency services for children and young people.	97
1997	First class delivery: improving maternity services in England and Wales.	112
1997	Health services for children and young people in the community: Health Committee 3rd report.	98
1997	Higher education in the learning society. (Dearing report)	73
1997	Hospital services for children and young people: Health Committee 5th report.	100
1997	Lecturer practitioner roles in England.	73
1997	NHS (Primary Care) Act 1997: chapter 46.	39
1997	The national visit.	118
1997	The new NHS: modern, dependable.	21
1997	Nurses, Midwives and Health Visitors Act 1997: chapter 24.	22
1997	Paediatric intensive care: a framework for the future.	100
1997	Patient's charter: mental health services.	117
1997	People like us.	101
1997	Preparation of supervisors of midwives.	111
1997	Pulling together: the future roles and training of mental health staff.	118
1997	Report on the review of patient identifiable information. (Caldicott report)	56
1997	The specific health needs of children and young people: Health Committee 2nd report.	98
1997	Voices in partnership: involving users and carers in commissioning and delivering mental health services.	119
1997	Witholding or withdrawing life saving treatment in children. (McIntosh report)	97
1998	Breaking the boundaries.	74
1998	Bringing Britain together: a national strategy for neighbourhood renewal.	43
1998	Community health care for elderly people. (Clark report)	84
1998	A consultation on a strategy for nursing, midwifery and health visiting.	22
1998	Creating lifelong learners.	112
1998	A first class service: quality in the new NHS.	57
1998	Guidelines for mental health and learning disability nursing.	129
1998	High hopes: making housing and community care work.	40
1998	Home alone: the role of housing in community care.	39
1998	Human Rights Act 1998: chapter 42.	58
1998	Ignored and invisible?	41
1998	Independent inquiry into inequalities in health. (Acheson report)	51
1998	Informal carers.	41

date	title	page
1998	In the public interest: developing a strategy for public participation in the NHS.	57
1998	Mental Health Act 1983: memorandum on parts I to IV, VIII and X.	120
1998	Midwifery: delivering our future. (Norman report)	112
1998	Modernising mental health services: safe, sound and supportive.	120
1998	Modernising social services: promoting independence, improving protection, raising standards.	41
1998	Our healthier nation: a contract for health.	50
1998	Partnership in action: new opportunities for joint working between health and social services: a discussion document.	42
1998	Public Interest Disclosure Act 1998: chapter 23.	58
1998	The regulation of nurses, midwives and health visitors: report on a review of the Nurses, Midwives and Health Visitors Act 1997. (J.M. Consulting)	23
1998	Signposts for success in commissioning and providing health services for people with learning disabilities.	129
1998	Standards for specialist education and practice.	74
1998	Tackling drugs to build a better Britain: the government's ten year strategy for tackling drug misuse.	119
1998	That bit of help: the high value of low level preventative services for older people.	84
1998	Tomorrow's nurses and midwives.	75
1998	Youth matters.	102
1999	Accountable care: developing the General Social Care Council.	60
1999	Better care, higher standards: a charter for long term care.	59
1999	Caring about carers: a national strategy for carers.	44
1999	Code of practice: Mental Health Act 1983.	121
1999	Cover story: the use of locum doctors in NHS trusts.	24
1999	Disability Rights Commission Act 1999: chapter 17.	130
1999	Facing the facts.	129
1999	First assessment: a review of district nursing services in England and Wales.	43
1999	Fitness for practice. (Peach report)	76
1999	The Health Act 1999: chapter 8.	24
1999	Healthcare futures 2010.	75
1999	A higher level of practice.	25
1999	Me, survive out there?	104
1999	Mental health nursing: addressing acute concerns. (Bell report)	122
1999	National service framework for mental health: modern standards and service models.	123

date	title	page
1999	Not because they are old: an independent inquiry into the care of older people on acute wards in general hospitals.	85
1999	Nursing in secure environments.	123
1999	Opportunity for all: tackling poverty and social exclusion.	44
1999	Protecting children, supporting parents.	103
1999	Protection of Children Act 1999: chapter 14.	104
1999	Review of prescribing, supply and administration of medicines. (Crown report)	25
1999	RCN mental health nursing strategy.	120
1999	Safer services. (Appleby report)	121
1999	Saving lives: our healthier nation.	51
1999	Small fortunes: spending on children, childhood poverty and parental sacrifice.	102
1999	Supporting doctors, protecting patients.	60
1999	With respect to old age: long-term care, rights and responsibilities. (Sutherland report)	85
1999	Working together to safeguard children.	103
2000	Adopting changes: survey and inspction of local councils' adoption services.	105
2000	Adoption: a new approach.	106
2000	Care Standards Act 2000: chapter 14.	45
2000	Children (Leaving Care) Act 2000: chapter 35.	105
2000	Comprehensive critical care: a review of adult critical care services.	25
2000	Excellence not excuses: inspection of services for ethnic minority children and families.	46
2000	Forget me not: mental health services for older people.	87
2000	Fully equipped: the provision of equipment to older or disabled people in England and Wales.	86
2000	Health service of all the talents: developing the NHS workforce.	77
2000	The last straw: explaining the NHS nursing shortage.	26
2000	Meeting the challenge: a strategy for allied health professions.	26
2000	New life for health. (Hutton report)	28
2000	The NHS plan: a plan for investment; a plan for reform.	27
2000	The NHS plan: the Government's response to the Royal Commission on Long Term Care.	86
2000	Nine to thirteen: the forgotten years.	105
2000	The nursing, midwifery and health visiting contribution to the continuing care of people with mental health problems.	123
2000	An organisation with a memory: report of an expert group on learning from adverse events in the NHS.	61

date	title	page
2000	Poverty and social exclusion in Britain.	46
2000	A quality strategy for social care.	61
2000	Reforming the Mental Health Act parts 1 and 2.	124
2000	Shaping the future NHS: long term planning for hospitals and related services.	28
2000	Social inequalities 2000 edition.	47
2000	Strategies for living.	124
2000	Vision 2000.	113
2000	The way to go home: rehabilitation and remedial services for older people.	87
2000	Your guide to the NHS.	62
2001	Brief encounters: getting the best from temporary nursing staff.	29
2001	Building a safer NHS for patients.	67
2001	Change here!: managing change to improve local services.	47
2001	Developing quality to protect children.	106
2001	Educating and training the future health professional workforce for England.	78
2001	Establishing the new Nursing and Midwifery Council.	66
2001	A fair deal for older people: public views on the funding of long-term care.	87
2001	Future imperfect? Report of the King's Fund Care and Support inquiry.	47
2001	Harold Shipman's clinical practice 1974 – 1998. (Baker report)	62
2001	Hidden talents: education, training & development for healthcare staff in NHS trusts.	77
2001	Information for social care.	67
2001	Making the change: a strategy for the professions in healthcare science.	29
2001	National Health Service Reform and Health Care Professions Bill 2001.	31
2001	National service framework for older people.	88
2001	National strategy for sexual health and HIV.	53
2001	National taskforce on violence against social care staff.	30
2001	Public health: House of Commons Health Committee 2nd report.	52
2001	Reference guide to consent for examination or treatment.	63
2001	Removal, retention and use of human organs and tissue from post-mortem examination: advice from the CMO.	65
2001	The report of the Chief Medical Officer's project to strengthen the public health function	53
2001	The report of the public inquiry into children's heart surgery: learning from Bristol	64
2001	Shifting the balance of power within the NHS: securing delivery.	30
2001	Skill mix in primary care: implications for the future.	48
2001	Tackling obesity in England: report by the Comptroller and Auditor General.	52

date	title	page
2001	Valuing people: a new strategy for learning disability for the 21st century.	130
2001	Voices, values and health: involving the public in moral decisions.	66
2001	Working together, learning together: a framework for lifelong learning in the NHS.	78
2002	Getting ahead of the curve: a strategy for combating infectious diseases (including other aspects of health protection).	54
2002	Old habits die hard: tackling age discrimination in health and social care.	88
2002	Omnibus survey about attitudes to the elderly in the UK.	89

1 General

Department of Health (1989) *Working for patients: the health service: caring for the 1990s (cm 555).* London: HMSO

Summary: a white paper that proposes seven key measures with the aim of giving patients greater choice and of increasing efficiency. The seven measures would implement reforms in the following areas:

- responsibility at local level
- self-governing trusts
- purchasers/providers being able to offer and receive services in other health authorities, with funding crossing administrative boundaries
- an increase consultant posts to reduce waiting times
- GP fundholding
- a streamlining of management structure based on regions introducing executive and non-executive directors
- to introduce medical audit to ensure quality of services is maintained

The document followed the Conservative Government's review of the NHS and introduced the most radical reforms in the NHS since its foundation in 1948.

Further reading:
Horne, E. M. (1989) Working for patients: begging the questions?....future management of the NHS. *Professional Nurse* 4(7) 318
Wheeler, N. (1990) "Working for patients" and "Caring for people" the same philosophy? *British Journal of Occupational Therapy* 53(10) 409-14

Department of Health (1989) *A strategy for nursing: a report of the steering committee.* London: Department of Health

Summary: looks at the challenges facing nursing in the new NHS, particularly in relation to the government policies stated in *Working for patients (1989)*. The report concentrates on practice, manpower, education, leadership and management and sets targets for these key areas.

Department of Health (1990) *The National Health Service and Community Care Act 1990: chapter 19.* London: HMSO

Summary: the first legislative reform of the NHS since its founding in 1948. Arises from the two white papers: *Working for patients (1989)* and *Caring for people (1991)*. Makes five key points:

1. QUALITY: as the result of the introduction of market forces, there should be explicit standards of care and patient information (Patient's charter 1991); measurable outcomes and evidence-based practice.
2. FLEXIBILITY: this legislates for the concept of a NEEDS-led service instead of the other way around. Health services to be redeveloped to suit needs of individuals, communities and populations.
3. CHOICE: purchasers of health services - eg GP fundholders - free to choose from a range of providers.
4. ACCOUNTABILITY: to establish who is responsible for delivering what health care: the responsibilities of the various care-giving agencies to be properly defined.
5. PARTNERSHIP: this is to legislate for good cooperation between: hospital and community agencies, statutory, voluntary and independent organisations, and between patients, professionals and informal carers.

Department of Health (1992) *Nurses, Midwives and Health Visitors Act 1992: chapter 16.* London: HMSO

Summary: this revises and updates the *Nurses, Midwives and Health Visitors Act 1979* altering the nature of the UKCC and National Boards to give the profession a further step towards self-regulation. The Act enables the professions to elect the majority of their representatives directly onto the UKCC, whilst reducing the size and role of the National Boards. National Board members to be appointed by the Secretary of State. The Act gives the UKCC greater responsibility in enforcing standards of professional conduct by allowing them sole responsibility.

Further reading:
Hempel, S. What do they do? a wide body (function of the ENB)
Nursing Times 90(10) 45.
Mangan, P. What do they do? registered approval (function of the UKCC)
Nursing Times 90(7) 51.
Professional Priorities...new Nurses, Midwives & Health Visitors Act. (1992)
Nursing Times 88(13) 20-21.

Department of Health (1993) *Report on the taskforce on the strategy for research in nursing, midwifery and health visiting.* (chair Adrian Webb) London: Department of Health

Summary: considers the role of research in the nursing profession. In particular the report concentrates on: identifying key research areas; examining education and training; discussing dissemination of funding and careers in research.

Further reading:
Hopps, L. C. (1994) The development of research in the United Kingdom.
Journal of Clinical Nursing 3(4) 199-204
Read, S. (1994) The strategy for research in nursing in England: initial impact.
Nurse Researcher 1(3) 72-84

Wright, S. (ed) (1993) *The named nurse, midwife and health visitor.*
London: Department of Health

Summary: accounts by health professionals in different settings of their experiences of the named nurse concept, which was introduced as part of the *Patient's charter (1991)*. Includes those working in acute and community units, learning disabilities, nursing homes, school nurses, midwives and many others. The editor's introduction highlights areas such as qualifications of nursing staff, workloads, teamwork and professional development in relation to the named nurse.

Further reading:
Boyington, J. (1992) The implementation of named nursing. *Nursing Standard* 7(2) 35-8
Jack, B. (1995) Using the named nurse system to improve patient care. *Nursing Times* 91(44) 34-35
Melville, E. (1995) The implementation of the named nurse concept. *Professional Nurse* 10(12) 800-801

NHS Management Executive (1993) *A vision for the future: the nursing, midwifery and health visiting contribution to health and health care.*
London: Department of Health

Summary: examines where the nursing profession fits into recent government changes in the NHS, with particular reference to quality, audit, accountability, clinical leadership, research, supervision and education. Identifies twelve key target areas for the professions. Relates policy implications of the four key docuemnts: *Children Act (1989), Caring for people (1991), Health of the nation (1992)* and the *Patient's charter (1991)*.

Further reading:
Mackereth, P. A. (1994) A vision for the future part 2: targets 5-9. *Nursing Standard* 8(50) 29-32
Mackereth, P. A. (1994) A vision for the future part 3: targets 10-12. *Nursing Standard* 8(51) 28-31
Wright, S. G. (1994) A vision for the future part 1: targets 1-4. *Nursing Standard* 8(49) 30-34

Greenhalgh & Co. (1994) *The interface between junior doctors and nurses: a research study for the Department of Health.* (chair Kenneth Calman) Macclesfield: Greenhalgh & Co.

Summary: the aim of the research was "to contribute to the improvement in patient care by examining the interface between junior hospital doctors and ward nurses, with a view to enhancing the role of nurses and reducing the inappropriate role of junior hospital doctors."

The researchers looked at three areas:
- what junior doctors do
- what work is transferable between junior doctors and nurses for the benefit of patients
- areas of good practice

The report recommends six activities that nurses should undertake emphasising that these "should be shared with junior doctors not merely transferred to nurses". These activities should be part of the role of all registered nurses and do not need to be undertaken by specialists or nurse practitioners.

These activities are:
- taking a patient history
- venous blood sampling
- insertion of a peripheral IV cannula
- referring a patient for an investigation
- writing discharge letters to GPs and other doctors
- administration of drugs (excluding cytotoxic and first doses) via peripheral IV cannula

The report suggests that joint planning of care and collaborative practice between junior doctors and nurses should be pursued. Joint education for practice and competency testing in the activities identified should be included in the core curriculum for pre-registration nursing and undergraduate medical training.

Further reading:
Richardson, G. and Maynard, A. (1995) *Fewer doctors? More nurses? A review of the knowledge base of doctor-nurse substitution. (Discussion paper 135)* York: University of York

Department of Health (1994) *The challenges for nursing and midwifery in the 21st century: the Heathrow debate.* London: Department of Health

Summary: series of discussions between chief nursing officers and other health professionals on the future role of nursing and midwifery, in the light of developments in government policy, technology and client needs. Areas examined include: care teams, nurses' role, cooperation with other caring professions, accountability, quality and training.

Audit Commission (1995) *The doctors' tale: the work of hospital doctors in England and Wales.* London: Audit Commission

Summary: the report presents a picture of doctors under increasing pressure owing to advances in technology, greater patient expectations and the need for efficiency; on the other hand doctors' work is often poorly defined, consultants' commitments are not clear, there is an uneven skill mix and workloads vary enormously often to the detriment of personal and family lives. Medical training is poorly organised and inflexible with insufficient supervision for junior doctors, many with no named supervisor. Recommendations include:
- clinical directors to take a lead role in managing doctors of all grades
- doctors' responsibilities to be made explicit, with "job" plans completed for all consultants and consideration given to work that could be passed to nurses or other staff

- service and training needs should be clearer and more structured: royal colleges to set standards of competence for trainees and trusts to write policies for doctors' professional development
- working practices should be more efficient with greater use of shifts in order to reduce the working hours of junior doctors and to allow for doctors who have family commitments

Further reading:
Butler, P. (1995) A sting in the tale. *Health Service Journal* 105(5444) 11
Sims, J. (1995) Will job plans stop the spying? *Healthcare Management* 3(4) 16-8

Department of Health (1996) *The National Health Service: a service with ambitions (cm 3425).* London: The Stationery Office

Summary: the Government outlines the fundamental principles on which the NHS was founded and restates its continued commitment to them. To these principles is added the requirement for a responsive and sensitive service in which the needs of the individual are met. Through a series of case studies, the Government demonstrates the kind of care that people should expect if the government's ambitions are to be realised. This will come about by setting five strategic objectives namely: a well-informed public, a seamless service, knowledge-based decision-making, a highly trained and skilled workforce and a responsive service.

The paper states that future pressures on the NHS such as medical advances, population changes and public expectations are manageable: the NHS has adapted and continues to adapt to change. Finally, the paper details several specific areas which need to be addressed. These are in the area of primary care (see Chapter 2), professional development and the provision of information.

Further reading:
News focus. (1996) *Health Service Journal* 106(5528) 12-13

Department of Health (1997) *The new NHS: modern, dependable (cm 3807).* London: The Stationery Office

Summary: white paper stressing the importance of primary care. The government proposes substantial savings (£1billion) on administrative costs, to be transferred directly to patient care, by replacing the internal market with "integrated care". This is to be achieved by the following initiatives:
- quality and efficiency to be improved and monitored by a National Institute for Clinical Excellence, setting evidence-based guidelines for clinicians. Some issues raised here are developed in *A first class service (1998)*
- introduction of Primary Care Groups (PCGs) made up of GPs and community nurses, to commission services from NHS Trusts on a long-term rather than annual basis. These PCGs replace fundholder groups
- fewer health authorities covering larger areas

The separation of planning and provision of care will continue.

Major developments in direct services to patients are:
1. NHS Direct, a 24-hour telephone advice service staffed by nurses, to be implemented nationally by 2000
2. all GPs connected to NHS Net by 2002 to speed up both booking of outpatient appointments and patients' results
3. improved cancer services with specialist appointments within 2 weeks of referral, to be implemented by 2000

Further reading:
Crail, M. (1997) Modern times. *Health Service Journal* 107(5583) 10-11
Crofts, L. (1998) Good news down the line. *Nursing Times* 94(28) 34-36
Keighley T (1998) Yvonne Moores. *Nursing Management* 4(10) 17-20
News: the NHS white paper (1997) *Nursing Standard* 12 (13/15) 36-37
Payne, D. (1997) Primary movers. *Nursing Times* 95(51) 8-9

Nurses, Midwives and Health Visitors Act 1997: chapter 24.
London: The Stationery Office

Summary: legislation that defines the constitution and responsibilities of the UKCC and the four national boards. The Act also legislates for the admission to and removal from the UKCC register, including the admission of European members. Provisions for midwifery include their supervision by local health authorities; regulations as to how midwives may practice; and outlawing the attendance of a woman in childbirth by a non-professional. This is a consolidation of the Acts of 1992 and 1979.

NHS Executive (1998) *A consultation on a strategy for nursing, midwifery and health visiting (HSC 1998/045).*
London: Department of Health

Summary: a consultation document preparing nurses, midwives and health visitors for the implementation of *The new NHS, modern, dependable (1997)* and *Our healthier nation (1998)*. Issues for consideration come under the headings: improving health, improving health care and *Vision for the future (1993)*, seen in the settings: school (child care), workplace (adult) and neighbourhoods (elderly).

- improving health: consideration to be given to different working methods to promote interagency working; new models of leadership based on the job to be done rather than on hierarchy; adopting a public health (rather than individual) approach to health promotion; development of school nurses and health visitors; influencing the production of Health Improvement Plans
- improving health care: while putting the patient at the centre of the care process, consideration given to how nurses may assume a greater role in health care planning; contribute to the primary care groups and to the production of the Health Improvement Plans; promote good parenting and stable families; act so as to command public support and respect; support or take a lead in clinical research; contribute to or lead the use of clinical governance

The report recognises that nurses need protection from stress, racism and violence and that they need flexible working arrangements. With regard to *Vision for the future (1993)*: there should be discussion about what may be kept, developed or discarded.

Further reading:
Bagnall, Pippa (1998) Consultation on a strategy for nursing. *British Journal of Community Health Nursing* 3(6) 268

J. M. Consulting (1998) *The regulation of nurses, midwives and health visitors: report on a review of the Nurses, Midwives and Health Visitors Act 1997.* Bristol: J.M. Consulting Ltd

Summary: as an independent consultancy, J.M. Consulting were commissioned by the Department of Health to review the most recent legislation governing the profession. The review was achieved by extensive consultation with the statutory bodies (UKCC and the four national boards) and with individuals, focus groups and representatives from nurse education providers. The main areas of concern are:

- protecting patients from unsafe practices
- new training arrangements and nurses' changing role
- accountability
- political devolution in the UK

The report identifies weaknesses and omissions in the legislation and recommends a new Act to regulate the professions with following recommendations:

- a new, single body to replace the UKCC and 4 national boards
- to improve standards, parity of representation for both nursing and midwifery
- the inclusion of lay advisors to assist the work of the new body
- a revised code of conduct
- the abolition of separate registration for health visitors
- the four UK health departments to regulate the training and practice of health care support workers

In February 1999, the Government publicly endorsed the review's recommendations but maintain that health visitors should continue to have separate registration.

Further reading:
Chaffer, D. (1998) Learn about plans for the health service tomorrow.
Nursing Standard 12(24 No Limits supplement) 49
Downe, S. (1998) Legislation and professional autonomy: is there a conflict?
British Journal of Midwifery 6(4) 234
Keighley, T. (1998) Structuring health care for the future.
Nursing Management 5(3) 23-7
Lewis, Paul (1999) Review of the Nurses, Midwives and Health Visitors Act.
British Journal of Midwifery 7(4) 214-5

Audit Commission (1999) *Cover story: the use of locum doctors in NHS trusts.* London: Audit Commission

Summary: on a typical day, 3,500 locums are employed to cover job vacancies, annual and sick leave at a cost of £214 million per annum. This can lead to problems of care because:

- with short postings (often less than two days), the locum may have only a poor induction to the setting and its procedures
- some locums have not held a permanent post for some time and their education and training may not be up-to-date
- pre-employment checks are not thorough

This can lead to unnecessary expense because agencies pay more per hour and trusts' systems for employing locums are inconsistent and poorly managed. Systems are open to fraud. Recommendations include:

- an accreditation system to ensure locums are working to a high standard
- all locums to be assured of an individual performance review (IPR)
- trusts to appoint a senior doctor to lead and be accountable for all doctors employed in this way
- for better value for money, trusts to set up contracts with agencies

The Health Act 1999: chapter 8. London: The Stationery Office

Summary: principally a reform of primary care, replacing GP fundholding with primary care trusts.

- outlines the functions of primary care trusts and their mechanisms for funding and expenditure
- primary care and NHS trusts to establish a "duty of quality" to monitor and improve the quality of health care
- a Commission for Health Improvement (CHI) will provide advice and information to trusts about meeting their duty of quality
- the CHI will have the power to carry out reviews and investigations into the management, availability and quality of care and (subject to regulation) may inspect premises, inspect and take copies of any documentation and publish without consent if there is considered to be risk to the welfare of patients. Subject to regulation the CHI may also charge the bodies responsible for the cost of the CHI's investigation
- Health Authorities and Trusts must work collaboratively
- Health Authorities to draw up Health Improvement Programmes; Local Authorities and NHS trusts to cooperate

The Act gives the Health Secretary the power to curb drug prices. It also legislates to modernise professional self-regulation: by-passing the customary parliamentary debate, the Act gives the Health Secretary the power to alter professional regulation.

Further reading:
Whitfield, Lyn (1999) After Henry. *Health Service Journal* 109(5641) 10-11.

UKCC (1999) *A higher level of practice: report of the consultation on the UKCC's proposals for a revised regulatory framework for post-registration clinical practice.* London: UKCC

Summary: discusses proposals for setting and regulating a generic standard for a higher level of practice with a system for assessment and with a charge levied for the assessment process.

Department of Health (1999) *Review of prescribing, supply and administration of medicines: final report.* (chair June Crown) London: Department of Health

Summary: after outlining the present situation of who may prescribe, supply and administer drugs, the report proposes extending prescribing powers and setting criteria for approving, training and regulating new prescribers. Defines two kinds of prescribers. The "independent" prescriber has the first contact with the patient and is responsible for the initial assessment, diagnosis and prescription. The "dependent" prescriber is responsible for the continuing care of the patient and may vary the frequency and dose of the original prescription. Good communication between the two parties is essential and to be regulated. The prime motivation of the report is improved patient care and an increase of patient choice.

Further reading:
Department of Health (1989) *Report of the advisory group on nurse prescribing.* London: Department of Health
Karen Luker et al (1997) *Evaluation of nurse prescribing: final report.* Liverpool: The University of Liverpool
Edwards, M. (1999) The Crown report: a new prescribing framework.
British Journal of Community Health Nursing 4(5) 212

Department of Health (2000) *Comprehensive critical care: a review of adult critical care services.* London: Department of Health

Summary: a three-five year modernisation programme. Proposals are made for every sector involved in critical care with examples of good practice. The existing division into high dependency and intensive care to be replaced by a classification that identifies four levels of care and can identify specialties such as renal, thoracic, surgical etc.

Critical care services should feature four characteristics:
- integration: there should a hospital-wide approach to critical care with support and communication between all the involved agencies
- networks: several trusts to integrate their services, working to common standards to provide the full range of critical care services within a geographical area
- workforce development: there should a planned approach to all personnel issues including education and training and involving all levels of staff
- data collecting culture promoting an evidence base: effective information gathering promotes good patient outcomes and turns a reactive service into a proactive one

Further reading:
Audit Commission (1999) *Critical to success: the place of efficient and effective critical care services within the acute hospital.* London: Audit Commission
Hogan, J. (2000) Staff ratios in intensive care: are they adequate? *British Journal of Nursing* 9(13) 817
Wright, Mike (2000) Intensive pressure. *Nursing Times* 96(33) 29-30

Meadows, S. Levenson, Ros and Baeza, Juan (2000) *The last straw: explaining the NHS nursing shortage.* London: King's Fund

Summary: the result of a literature review and a series of interviews and focus groups with NHS nurses and managers. Nurses are leaving the NHS faster than they are being recruited: of a total workforce of 330,000, the shortfall is estimated to be between 8,000 and 13,000. Reasons given:

- low pay
- bleak working conditions
- lack of control
- discrimination and harrassment of black and ethnic minority workers

The authors recommend:

- managers to listen to nurses
- ensuring career development for all
- eliminating discrimination
- offering support and flexible working hours

Further reading:
Audit Commission (1997) *Finders keepers: the management of staff turnover in NHS trusts.* London: Audit Commission
Carvel, John (2001) NHS recruitment: search for staff to fulfill health pledges. *The Guardian* 23.5.01
Davies, J. (2000) Finders, keepers. *Health Service Journal* 110(5733) 24-9
Audit Commission (2001) *Brief encounters: getting the best from temporary nursing staff.* London: Audit Commission (see below)

NHS Executive (2000) *Meeting the challenge: a strategy for allied health professions.* London: Department of Health

Summary: a strategy designed to bring allied health professionals (such as podiatrists, radiographers, speech therapists etc) into line with the rest of health and social care services as part of *The NHS plan: a plan for investment, a plan for reform (2000).* The strategy allows a four-year timescale and includes the following proposals:

- changes to be overseen by an Allied Health Professions forum
- workforce to expand from 50,000 to 60,000 and to include new Consultant Therapist posts by 2004
- services to be made faster and more accessible
- improve care for in heart disease, cancer and mental illnesses and for older people

- care to be patient-focused and protocol-based
- improve interagency communication within health and social care services
- professions to be regulated by a Health Professions Council with a single register

Department of Health (2000) *The NHS plan: a plan for investment; a plan for reform (cm4818-I).* London: The Stationery Office

Summary: a ten-year plan promising financial investment for:
- personnel – 7,500 more consultants, 2,000 more GPs, 20,000 more nurses
- beds – 7,000 more by 2004
- cleaner hospitals – 'clean up' campaign to start immediately
- equipment for cancer, kidney and heart disease services
- a National Performance Fund
- twenty diagnostic and treatment centres for day and short stay surgery
- hospitals – 100 new hospitals by 2010 as well as 500 primary care centres

The reforms include:
- contracts that commit consultants to working up to seven years for the NHS with reward for further commitment
- faster access: by 2005, waiting times for operations to be reduced to six months and outpatient appointments to three months. Where an operation is cancelled for non-clinical reasons, patient to be funded for a private operation
- nurses to gain greater prescribing powers as well as the power to admit and discharge patients
- a new level of Primary Care Trusts to commission total health and social care packages
- Community Health Councils to be replaced by patient advocacy services and patient forums
- a national framework for working in the private sector
- the appointment of senior sisters ('modern matrons') in hospitals to control resources in order to improve standards of care. They will have the authority to intervene to sort out discharge delays and poor hygiene
- nurse consultant posts increased to 1000
- special improvements in services for care of patients with heart disease, cancer and mental illness as well as elderly people

Further reading:
Castledine, George (2000) Reinforcing the medical stereotypes of nursing. *British Journal of Nursing* 9(15) 1026
Scott, Helen (2000) Nursing has a chance to stop the erosion of care. *British Journal of Nursing* 9(15) 960
Anon (2000) The national plan for the NHS: your essential guide. *Nursing Times* 96(31) 4-7

Commission on the National Health Service (2000) *New life for health.* (chair Will Hutton) London: Vintage

Summary: this report was commissioned by the Association of Community Health Councils for England and Wales and is the result of a study of the NHS including a telephone poll of the public conducted in March 2000.

The poll:
- 63% believed the NHS was our most valuable institution
- 60% felt the NHS needed improvement
- 96% believed that free medical treatment at the time of need – the basic tenet of the NHS since its inception – should be a basic British right

The Commission found that by any standards, service delivery in the NHS is very low and that there is a growing gap between delivery and expectation. The 3 main reasons for this are:

1. low finance has meant that some services such as dentistry and long-term care are not always available on the NHS
2. the internal market led to inequality of care, although the establishment of NICE and the CHI has gone some way to remedy this
3. an absence of accountability and "transparent" decision-making: there is no solid "settled" system of patient rights, the NHS bill for medical negligence currently stands at £3billion, overall the NHS ethos is defensive and based on blame

The Commission makes two radical recommendations:

1. the Government to consult the public in writing a constitution for the NHS that would represent shared principles irrespective of party politics
2. the NHS to become a national institution similar to the BBC or the Bank of England: independent of government control but with Government having overall "arm's length" responsibility

Further reading:
Watt, N. (2000) Ministers should let go control of the NHS. *The Guardian* 18.4.00
Miles, Alice (2000) Patients do not have a cure for the NHS. *The Times* 25.4.00

Department of Health (2000) *Shaping the future NHS: long term planning for hospitals and related services: consultation document on the findings of the National Bed Inquiry.* London: The Stationery Office

Summary: the National Beds Inquiry was set up to look at the hospital beds situation ten to twenty years ahead. Concerns about the pressures on emergency beds during the winter and the length of hospital waiting lists led to the establishment of the Inquiry. It has three aims:

- to investigate the key resources needed by the NHS in the long term, and to assess the future impact of current policies and other factors, taking into account the wider picture
- to consult with the NHS and partner agencies about these investigations and involve them in discussions about developments (especially about hospital beds) over the next 10 to 20 years

- to assist with long-term planning by producing a common set of assumptions from their findings

Audit Commission (2001) *Brief encounters: getting the best from temporary nursing staff.* London: Audit Commission

Summary: on any single day, 20,000 bank or agency nurses are employed to cover sick leave, job vacancies, annual leave and to a much lesser extent, study and maternity leave. This can lead to poor quality care because nurses are assigned to unfamiliar settings, inductions and handovers are rarely given and pre-employment checks are not thoroughly carried out (e.g. work permits, UKCC registration, occupational health checks and police records). The situation presents poor value for money because time is wasted due to poor planning, agencies commonly pay 20-25% more than nursing banks and the systems for filling in timesheets and claims forms are open to fraud and exploitation. Recommendations include:

- to ensure pre-employment checks are made and inductions properly given
- to ensure all temporary staff receive basic training, especially in emergency procedures, lifting and handling etc and to support bank staff's applications for training
- to ensure proper control of timesheets and payment claims
- trusts to open contracts with agencies
- to ensure more cost effective and less reactive staff planning, with central coordination of staff cover and standardised processes that make better use of information technology

Further reading:
Mahony, Chris et al (2001) Watchdog's verdict: millions squandered, nurses neglected: Nursing Times special feature. *Nursing Times* 97(36) 10-13

NHS Executive (2001) *Making the change: a strategy for the professions in healthcare science.* London: Department of Health

Summary: a four-year plan designed to raise standards on the one hand and on the other, raise the public profile and working conditions of health care scientists. The different professions included in health care science are described and the plan's proposals include:

- the development of a National Occupational Standards Framework in healthcare science to define best practice and direct education and training
- to replace the Council for Professions Supplementary to Medicine with a new Health Professions Council and a single Health Professions Register
- enhance public confidence by raising healthcare scientists' profiles
- modernise education and training and improve healthcare science career opportunities in order to raise standards and resolve problems with recruitment and retention

Department of Health (2001) *Shifting the balance of power within the NHS: securing delivery.* London: Department of Health

Summary: as an extension of the *NHS plan (2000)* this consultation paper plans for the reform of managment by shifting emphasis to "frontline" staff working in the community. The four main points are:

1. Primary Care Trusts (PCTs) to become the lead organisation in assessing, planning and commissioning health services and to work at new partnerships with local agencies and local government. Resources to be allocated directly to the Trusts rather than via Health Authorities.
2. NHS Trusts to continue to provide services whilst devolving responsibility to clinical teams and promoting clinical networks across the NHS. High performance to be rewarded.
3. The 95 local Health Authorities to be replaced by 30 Strategic Health Authorities that will look at the strategic development of health services as well as performance and accountability of the Trusts.
4. Department of Health Regional Offices to be replaced by four Directors of Health and Social Care, overseers who will provide the link between the NHS and the Department of Health. NHS staff and services to be supported by three new bodies: The Modernisation Agency, the Leadership Centre and the University of the NHS.

If passed, the *NHS Reform and Health Care Professions Bill 2001* will legislate for the proposed changes.

Further reading:
Editorial (2001) Shifting the furniture: yet more upheaval.
Health Service Journal 111(5766) 17
Bamford, Terry et al (2001) Thoughts on shifting the balance of power.
British Journal of Health Care Management 7(9) 355-7
Graham, Alison and Steele, Jane (2001) *Optimising value.* London: Public Management Foundation
Walshe, Kieran and Smith, Judith (2001) Cause and effect.
Health Service Journal 111(5776) 20-3

Department of Health (2001) *National taskforce on violence against social care staff: report and national action plan.* London: The Stationery Office

Summary: the Task Force was set up in September 1999 and the theme of this report is the unacceptability of any form of violence, physical or verbal, against social care staff or service users. The remit of the Task Force was to:

- reduce substantially all violence against social workers in social care settings and to set up systems to sustain this reduction
- produce a National Action Plan by November 2000, recommending measures to promote the welfare and safety of all social care workers
- set up a training initiative with the Department of Health
- set up targets for the reduction of violence and to monitor progress

- help social care workers to develop strategies to reduce violence and offer training in handling difficult situations
- support victims of violence in social care
- start a programme for management to develop guidelines and good practice

The report states that it is the legal and moral duty of employers to safeguard their social care staff and notes that this should improve the service for the users and improve efficiency all round.

Further reading:
Winchester, R. (2000) Task force seeks to highlight anti-violence agenda. *Community Care* 14.12.00 10-11

National Health Service Reform and Health Care Professions Bill 2001. London: The Stationery Office

Summary: a bill to provide for:
- the reforming and financial arrangements of Health Authorities, PCTs and other health bodies in England and Wales
- further functions of the Commission for Health Improvement
- the functions of patients' forums, the Commission for Patient and Public Involvement in Health with the abolition of the Community Health Councils in England
- the Council for the Regulation of Health Care Professionals
- the regulation of pharmacists
- appeals procedures for medical professionals, dentists, opticians, osteopaths and chiropractors

Supplementary Reading

Audit Commission (2001) *A spoonful of sugar: medicines management in NHS hospitals.* London: Audit Commission

Audit Commission (1992) *Making time for patients: a handbook for ward sisters.* London: HMSO

Beardshaw, V. and Robinson, R. (1990) *New for old? prospects for nursing in the 1990s (research report no. 8).* London: King's Fund Institute

Coker, Naaz (ed) (2001) *Racism in medicine: an agenda for change.* London: King's Fund

Comptroller and Auditor General (2002) *NHS Direct in England.* (HC505 Session 2001-2002) London: The Stationery Office

Data Protection Act 1984: chapter 35. London: HMSO

Harrison, Anthony (2001) *Making the right connections: the design and management of health care delivery.* London: King's Fund

Kingsley, Sue and Pawar, Asha (2002) *Putting race equality to work in the NHS: a resource for action.* London: Department of Health

NHS Executive (2000) *Workforce and development: embodying leadership in the NHS.* London: NHSE

Performance and Innovation Unit, Cabinet Office (2001) *Strengthening leadership in the public sector: a research study.* London: PIU

Race Relations (Amendment) Act 2000: chapter 34. London: The Stationery Office

Toynbee, Polly and Walker, David (2000) *Did things get better? An audit of Labour's successes and failures.* Harmondsworth: Penguin Books

2 Primary and Community Care

Audit Commission (1986) *Making a reality of community care.* London: HMSO

Summary: a report that states that although it is government policy to move away from long-term hospital care towards care in the community, the move is failing. While hospital care is being run down, community care is not keeping pace to fill the gap, especially in mental health; discrepancies are noted from one locality to another, again in mental health; the reduction in NHS hospitals has been met by an increase in private residential care, paid for by supplementary benefit at a cost of more than £500 million. The report's concern is that the money saved is being wasted and that some disabled and vulnerable people are missing out on care altogether. The following recommendations are offered:

- funding to be rationalised and short-term funds allowed to cover the transition period
- social service and community care policies to be coordinated to allow cooperation between the various agencies and a multi-disciplinary team approach to an individual's care
- local responsibilities, authority and accountability to be clearly defined
- local authorities given greater power
- staff training to be given to prepare them for community care
- provision made for cost-effective voluntary organisations
- to do nothing is absolutely untenable: the assets released from the rundown of hospitals were inadequately redeployed and a 37% increase in the elderly population is projected over the next ten years

Further reading:
Trnobranski, P. H. Implementation of community care policy in the United Kingdom: will it be achieved? *Journal of Advanced Nursing* 21(5) 988-95

DHSS (1986) *Neighbourhood nursing: a focus for care.* (chair Julia Cumberlege) London: HMSO

Summary: a report that offers a more effective way of planning community health care, based on needs. Suggests that within each health authority, neighbourhoods should be set up, each with a manager, to coordinate nurses, community midwives, psychiatric nurses, mental handicap nurses and specialist nurse practitioners even though they may be employed by and accountable to other bodies. Other proposals include:

- limited nurse-prescribing
- the primary health care team to have full, written understanding and support from GPs with the right to be informed of changes in an individual's care or treatment
- an end to general practice subsidies to employ district nurses

- developments in nurse education to prepare nurses for community work.
- an amalgamation of District Health Authorities and Family Practitioner Committees.

Further reading:
Cumberlege, J. (1986) Power to the people... neighbourhood nursing service. *Lampada* Summer (8) 16-18

DHSS (1987) *Promoting better health: the government's programme for improving primary health care (cm 249).* London: HMSO

Summary: white paper setting out the Government's plans for improving the primary health care services. Looks at changing the emphasis in primary care from the treatment of illness to the promotion of health and the prevention of disease, and sees health professionals as leading that change. Government objectives in this review of primary care services are:

- to make services more responsive to the needs of the consumer
- to raise standards of care
- to promote health and prevent illness
- to give patients the widest range of choice in obtaining high quality primary care services
- to improve value for money
- to enable clearer priorities to be set for Family Practitioner Services in relation to the rest of the NHS

Further reading:
Robinson, P. R. and Simon, T. (1988) Promoting better health: the government's programme for improving primary health care. *Physiotherapy* 74(4) 207

Department of Health (1988) *Community care: agenda for action.* (chair Roy Griffiths) London: HMSO

Summary: offers a plan for the care of adults in the community with a view to enabling individuals to receive the right care at the right time, to have a say and a choice in their care and where possible, to be cared for in their own homes.

Proposals:
- appointing a Minister of State with responsibility for community care
- that local social services should assess/identify needs of individuals and locality; arrange for the delivery of care; design, organise and purchase non-health care services; all in collaboration with health authorities and voluntary and private providers
- that local social services should have responsibility for funding
- that central government should arrange for the transfer of funds and provide a significant proportion of the total cost
- that local authorities should have adequate management systems in place

- that health authorities should have continued responsibility for medical community health care services with GPs responsible for making local authorities aware of particular needs
- that local and health authorities should have the power to act jointly or as agents for each other
- that the functions of a community carer develop into a new occupation with appropriate training so that one person can provide whatever help is needed. For this to happen there needs to be an understanding about the contribution of other professionals in the field to avoid insularity

Further reading:
Rayner, M. (1990) Two steps ahead of Griffiths...community care.
Nursing Times 86(15) 40-1
Shuttleworth, A. (1988) Whatever happened to the Griffiths Report? Community care.
Professional Nurse 4(3) 119-20

Department of Health (1989) *Caring for people: community care in the next decade and beyond (cm 849)*. London: HMSO

Summary: endorses the recommendations of the Griffiths report and sets out six key objectives:
- to promote domiciliary, day and respite services in order to enable people to live in their own homes
- practical support for carers to be a high priority
- the "cornerstone" of community care to be a proper assessment of need and good case management
- to encourage the independent sector - voluntary and private
- to clarify the various caring agencies' responsibilities
- to establish a new funding structure with no incentive given in favour of residential and nursing home care

The report recognises the continuing need for long-term hospital care; that primary health care workers are generally a patient's first port of call and that the voluntary sector need a clear role with a sounder financial base to allow them a greater degree of certainty.

Seven key changes are outlined:
- local authorities (LAs) to be responsible for assessing overall need, designing care arrangements and securing their delivery
- LAs to publish yearly plans for development
- LAs to make maximum use of the independent sector
- LAs to take responsibility for the financial support of people in residential and nursing homes
- applicants with no resources of their own to be eligible for the same levels of income support and housing benefit whether in their own or a nursing / residential home

- LAs to establish inspection and registration units to check on standards in their own and independent residential care homes
- a specific grant to be made available for the social care of the seriously mentally ill

Although the LAs are to take the lead responsibility, the report states that the Health Services must be responsible for maintaining good collaboration with Social Services and must contribute to the forming of the yearly community care plan.

Further reading:
Caring for people: community care. (1991) *Senior Nurse* 10(1) 1
Wheeler, N. (1990) "Working for patients" and "Caring for people": the same philosophy? *British Journal of Occupational Therapy* 53(10) 409-14

UKCC (1991) *Report on the proposals for the future of community education and practice.* London: UKCC

Summary: a report that identifies influences on community care nursing, with proposals for education and training.

Influences: Project 2000 and PREP, NHS reforms, links between health and social services; move towards health promotion and towards more community-based care.

- identifies range of needs that community health care nurses (CNs) must prepare for, such as health promotion and palliative care, and outlines ten broadly-defined core skills that include audit, support of informal carers and working within a multi-disciplinary team
- states that CNs will have qualifications and experience beyond those of newly qualified nurses and should take a leadership/management role within the community health care team
- states conditions for CN qualifications that include the need for modules to be inter/intradisciplinary and that courses be designed to meet core skills and a range of needs
- acknowledges existing qualifications of nurses such as district nurses and community psychiatric nurses.

North West Thames Regional Health Authority (1991) *Nursing in the community: report of the working group.* (chair Sheila Roy) London: HMSO

Summary: working group commissioned to see how managers and practitioners were responding to the white papers: *Promoting better health (1987)*; *Working for patients (1989)* and *Caring for people (1991)*. Suggests a shift in priorities towards a "health" rather than a "sickness" service; community care as a primary point of care and providing optimum care in the most cost-effective way. Outlines five possible organisational models and gives a series of checklists for the RHAs, DHAs, FHSAs, independent provider units, general practices and nurses.

Audit Commission (1992) *Homeward bound: a new course for community health.* London: HMSO

Summary: a review of community health services from government level to the workface that identifies the following weaknesses:
- lack of interprofessional cooperation
- lack of planned priority spending
- "patchwork" service as the result of poor overall management
- poorly planned skill mix and the need for greater "clarity in roles and procedures"
- poorly organised quality assurance.

Recommends: an "agenda for action" that looks at vision and need, strategic planning and the coordination of care.

NHS Management Executive (1993) *New world, new opportunities: report of a task group on nursing in primary health care.* London: HMSO

Summary: looks at developments in primary health care in the light of the white papers: *Caring for people (1989), The health of the nation (1992)* and the "contract culture of the reformed NHS"
- describes the opportunity to increase the range of skills in: health needs assessment, health promotion, treatment protocols and in a greater range of specialist services such as palliative care, diabetes care and rehabilitation
- suggests there is scope for nurses to enhance collaboration with other agencies and professionals and to extend their influence in the area of public health
- suggests the best way to meet the health care needs of individuals is to focus on the practice population, thus encouraging teamwork and collaboration
- suggests that while primary health care nurses have held a low profile in the past, the new developments will require them to enhance their clinical skills and levels of education

The report ends with 53 "keys to progess" i.e. suggestions of specific contributions.

Further reading:
Jackson, C. (1994) New world, new dilemmas: policy to integrate health visitors and district nurses with the primary health care team. *Health Visitor* 67(1) 8-9
Thompson, M. (1993) Brave new world? Future of community nursing and nurses suggests a broadening of clinical practice. *Nursing Standard* 7(28) 24

RCN Health Visitors Forum (1994) *Into the 90s: a discussion document on the future of health visiting practice.* London: Royal College of Nursing

Summary: aims to help health visitors negotiate their roles and status with current and future employers and offers four recommendations:
- health visiting to be seen as a collection of skills rather than a fixed role
- health visiting skills to be seen as applying to a range of client groups and settings
- health visitors to be proactive in the purchasing process

- block contracts and generic job descriptions to be dropped in favour of ones that match health visiting skills to local need.

Department of Health (1995) *Carers (Recognition and Services) Act 1995: chapter 12.* London: HMSO

Summary: this Act gives carers the right to request local authorities to assess their ability to provide adequate care and if necessary to provide additional resources to assist them in caring. The legislation formally recognises the care needs of disabled or elderly people at home, and the needs of their carers as well.

Further reading:
Andrews, J. (1995) Who cares for the carers? *Practice Nurse* 10(7) 450-1
George, M. (1995) Collaborative caring. *Nursing Standard* 9(46) 22-3
New act protects rights of carers. (1996) *Elderly Care* 8(3) 6

NHS Executive (1996) *Primary care: the future.* London: NHS Executive

Summary: the result of a listening exercise by the Minister for Health as part of a debate on primary health care. Patients, GPs, nurses, midwives and health visitors, pharmacists, optometrists, therapists and health service managers were invited to give their views on how primary care should develop. Five "touchstones" are noted: quality, fairness, accessibility, responsiveness and efficiency. Seven themes arise for an agenda:

- resources: the balance between primary and secondary provision is considered
- partnerships in care: to improve collaboration between agencies; the increasing role of the non-medical carer is noted
- developing professional knowledge: suggests a greater emphasis on a multidisciplinary approach
- patient and carer information and involvement: notes patient responsibilities as well as rights
- securing the workforce and premises: notes a different approach to GP and other professionals' contracts as well as improving the quality of actual physical premises
- better organisation: notes linking general practices together, reducing bureaucracy and developing information technology
- local flexibility

Contains a chapter on nurses, midwives and health visitors which stresses scope for extended role, greater managerial responsibility, joint education with GPs. There is concern for the isolation of practice nurses.

Further reading:
Buxton, V. (1996) Visions for the future: the future of primary care. *Nursing Times* 92(25) 26-7

Department of Health (1996) *Choice and opportunity: primary care: the future (cm 3390).* London: The Stationery Office.

Summary: a white paper that proposes a need for legislation that will encourage local flexibility in organisation, staffing and finance in order to deliver primary care services appropriate to local needs and circumstances. The paper concentrates on GPs, dentists, pharmacists and optometrists. The paper proposes legislation that will enable those who wish it to pilot different types of contract, for the appointment of GPs.

Further reading:
Cole, A. (1996) Opportunity knocks. *Health Visitor* 69(12) 484-5

Department of Health (1996) *Primary care: delivering the future.*
London: The Stationery Office

Summary: brings together themes raised in *Primary care: the future (1996)* and *The NHS: a service with ambitions (1996)*. Rather than radical change the paper proposes a direction for evolution towards a primary care-led NHS.

Aims and proposals:
- to enable local people to determine the service they want
- to coordinate all involved professionals: dentists, pharmacists, optometrists, social workers and housing officers as well as the primary health care team
- to improve professional development and knowledge-based decision-making
- to improve collaboration and cooperation so as to enable "seamless" management of care between organisations
- to improve the use of information technology
- patients to recognise their responsibility to the service as well as for their own health
- an increase in the proportion of goverment funding for primary care, including research and development funding
- practice staff to come in to the NHS Pension Scheme by September 1997
- to improve the range, quality and standard of work premises

National Health Service (Primary Care) Act 1997: chapter 46.
London: The Stationery Office

Summary: builds on the last two white papers and legislates to give nurses and GPs the right to set up and run pilot schemes for providing primary care services.

Further reading:
Thomas, S. (1997) Developing the primary care led NHS.
Journal of Community Nursing 11(6) 8-11

Audit Commission (1998) *Home alone: the role of housing in community care.* London: Audit Commission

Summary: a first document to point out the vital role played by housing services in the delivery of community care. The work of housing agencies includes: provision of social housing, adapting properties, provision of support for vulnerable clients, coordinating efforts with social services. There are four chapters:

1. 'Housing services' comprise alarms and adaptations; sheltered housing or with personal support for people with disabilities; resettling the homeless and offering

support to enable people to remain, coping in their own homes. Housing amounts to a "lower" level of support but serves a huge population, in greater numbers than health or social services. Their finance comes from central government, local housing departments, health authorities and social services, housing corporations and RSL. A crisis is emerging because with an increasing demand for the service, the stock of social housing has gone down, the role of housing authorities is changing and major changes in housing benefit are imminent.

2. Effective delivery is failing because of poor collaboration with health authorities and social services; inadequate identification of needs and poor planning: failure to intervene early enough is leading to a reactive approach to crises and delays.

3. Local level solutions would include: a system for gathering information about local needs; reviewing performance; awareness of provision and better use of resources.

4. At a national level: the funding regime needs overhauling: costs are shunted and there is poor information about the actual cost of services. Uncoordinated policies - eg the impact of closure of long-stay psychiatric facilities - lead to major problems in service delivery, and it is not clear "who owns the problems".

Watson, Lynn (1998) *High hopes: making housing and community care work.* London: Joseph Rowntree Foundation

Summary: following a series of research projects made between 1993 and 1996, this reports the following deficits in service:

- a "disconnection" between the messages of community care promoting independence and the reality of living in very poor quality accommodation
- whilst specialist housing is proven to be beneficial, there are huge differences in the level of housing provision from one locality to another
- well-planned accommodation can reduce the need for support, but this pay-off isn't always evident; the wait for an initial assessment can be more than 20 weeks and there isn't always the capital available to pay for the recommendations
- constraints on resources inhibit preventive strategies; many people do not qualify for help until their situation is critical
- at assessment, needs can go unrecorded because they fall outside certain criteria and clients are often in a weak position at the time (eg hospital discharge)
- in spite of having statutory rights, clients can be made to feel dependent and lacking in status; very few independent groups exist that offer advocacy
- planning services is difficult because of a difference in focus between the various agencies, having to meet performance indicators inhibits flexibility and because of continuous upheaval and shifts in agency responsibilities

The report ends with three recommendations:

- a major initiative to make effective use of housing stock and expansion of schemes of "care and repair" and to allow people to "stay put"
- to promote a needs-led service there should be national guidance on preventive support services
- independent advocacy and advice centres to be officially encouraged in order to help clients with making informed choices

Henwood, Melanie (1998) *Ignored and invisible? Carers' experience of the NHS: report of a UK research survey commissioned by the Carers National Association.* London: Carers National Association

Summary: the report gives the context of health policy under the Labour government followed by a profile of the 3,000 respondents to the survey. Subsequent sections examine:
- provision of support: most are caring alone with limited support from social services, district nursing and other home services such as chiropody. Those who received no support believed it would have been helpful
- many carers have health problems of their own, reporting physical injury and treatment for stress-related illness as the result of caring
- provision of information is inadequate and often has to be pushed for
- hospital discharge and after care arrangements are often poor
- NHS staff: GPs were rated highest, followed by district nurses; hospital social workers were not highly rated
- the top priorities for carers were: funding, cooperation between health and social services, the need for GPs to continue to make home visits and for all health staff to be trained in awareness of carers' needs

The chief recommendations are that pressure should be brought to bear on the NHS to meet the requirements of the *Carers (Recognition and Services) Act 1995* and on the Department of Health to take responsibility for improving the coherence of health and social care services.

Rowlands, Olwen (1998) *Informal carers: an independent study carried out by the Office for National Statistics on behalf of the Department of Health as part of the 1995 general household survey.*
London: The Stationery Office

Summary: a two-part report. Part 1 gives the results of questions on prevalence, who cares for whom and for how long, on time spent caring and who supports the carers. Part 2 reports on the trends since 1985: there has been little overall increase in numbers; there is a growing difference between those who are involved in heavy, full-time caring and those who offer a few hour's help; there is a decrease in the elderly's need for certain kinds of help such as mobility and self-care and overall, major care needs tend to emerge after the age of 75.

Department of Health (1998) *Modernising social services: promoting independence, improving protection, raising standards (cm 4169).*
London: The Stationery Office

Summary: long awaited reform that begins by noting six stumbling blocks to effective social care:
- protection: inadequate safeguards exist to protect the vulnerable
- coordination: conflict between authorities about who is to pay for what care

- inflexibility: help should be needs-led, not just what the service can offer
- role: clients don't know what help they can get from whom and to what standard
- inconsistency: uneven levels of service across the country
- inefficiency: great variations in cost from council to council

The plan for improvement includes seven proposals:
- adults: direct payments to people over 65 should support their need for independent living and give real control over provision of service. Social services to have nationally established objectives and priorities, regulating who gets what and conducting satisfaction surveys
- children: tougher inspection arrangements for their protection; funding for the "Quality Protects" programme to improve children's social services; improved educational opportunities for children in care as well as help with the transition to adulthood
- protection: new systems for protecting vulnerable children and adults including eight regional "Commissions for Care Standards"
- standards: a social care training strategy and the establishment of a "GSCC" - General Social Care Council - to set ethical standards and standards of practice
- partnerships with health: pooling budgets, improving partnerships with housing and other services
- improving delivery and efficiency: local authorities to be set targets, published annually, for quality and efficiency. Where standards are not met, central government to take action

Further reading:
Douglas, Anthony (1998) Motherhood and apple pie. *Community Care* 3.12.1998 12
Philpot, Terry (1998) Let history judge. *Community Care* 3.12.1998 18-20

Department of Health (1998) *Partnership in action: new opportunities for joint working between health and social services: a discussion document.* London: Department of Health

Summary: in order to promote joint working and remove barriers between health, social services and other local government agencies, the government's aims are:
- pooled budgets: allowing either agency to commission and provide services and compile integrated care packages
- appointing a single commissioning authority (local authority, health authority or primary care group) to be responsible for commissioning health or social care
- NHS or primary care trusts to provide social care services beyond their current powers and equally, social services to provide limited health services (such as chiropody) in contract with the NHS

The document proposes financial incentives to encourage joint working and measures to monitor and review the process that include: joint national priorities guidance, joint performance frameworks and consideration for bodies such as the Audit Commission to make joint inspections.

Social Exclusion Unit (1998) *Bringing Britain together: a national strategy for neighbourhood renewal (cm4045).* London: The Stationery Office

Summary: begins by describing how Britain has become a divided country with the poorest neighbourhoods locked into a downward spiral, becoming more rundown and more prone to social problems and unemployment. The strategy for renewal is based on investment in people and involving the whole community to provide solutions. The plan includes:

- tackling unemployment
- good housing and neighbourhood managment
- the Sure Start programme, improving prospects for young people
- improving access to basic services such as banks and shops

The strategy is to be coordinated by the Social Exclusion Unit for England and equivalent agencies for Wales, Scotland and Northern Ireland.

Further reading:
Alcock, P. (1998) Bringing Britain together? *Community Care* 26.11.1998 18-24
Frean, A. (1998) Blair heralds fight against urban squalor. *The Times* 16.9.1998 9
Hetherington, Peter (1998) Blair pledges programme to bridge growing gap between rich and poor. *The Guardian* 16.9.1998 6

Audit Commission (1999) *First assessment: a review of district nursing services in England and Wales.* London: Audit Commission

Summary: in the light of the major political changes as outlined in the white paper: *The New NHS: modern, dependable (1998)* and culminating in the formation of Primary Care Groups (PCGs) in April 1999, this report aims to provide a picture of the district nursing service with a view to helping PCGs in their decision-making. Having set the scene, the report divides into four chapters giving recommendations as follows:

1. Managing demand: needs should be identified and work objectives agreed with district nurses. There should be increased public awareness of the service and established criteria for referrals. There should be reviews of the discharge process as well as casemix and resourcing and regular review of nurses' own caseloads.

2. Improving quality: patient assessment should be improved; patients' views should be monitored and the information gained considered when determining changes. Clinical effectiveness would be increased by ensuring appropriate skill mix, developing clinical guidelines, encouraging local clinical audit and improving access to good clinical information. There should be promotion of peer review and support.

3. Improving the efficiency of the district nursing service: the process of monitoring skill and grade mix should be set against patient need and time of need. There should be increased development of professional education and training. The service should review the use of bank staff and seek to ensure they have regular training, delegating the bank staff budget to district nurse teams. The out-of-hours service should be improved: reviewing the need for a service, integrating day and evening services, possibly linking with the medical out-of-hours service. There should be greater development of drop-in and specialist district nurse clinics.

4. Aimed at managers, the last chapter repeats some of the previous points and adds the need for better coordination with social services; an improvement in the referral process and improved integration with other kinds of community nurses. The need for good leadership is stressed along with good team support and performance evaluation.

Further reading:
While, Alison (1999) District nurses need to define district nursing of the future. *British Journal of Community Health Nursing* 4(4) 203

Department of Social Security (1999) *Opportunity for all: tackling poverty and social exclusion (cm4445).* London: The Stationery Office

Summary: a white paper that outlines the extent of poverty and social exclusion in the UK and then describes a strategy to tackle the problem in four sections:
- children and young people
- people of working age
- older people
- communities

Based on three principles: *prevention* – tackling causes; *creating opportunity* and *empowerment* – investing in individuals, the strategy is to be long-term, flexible and collaborative. Recommendations include:
- investment in early years, education and help for families
- reducing teenage pregnancy
- helping people into employment, creating employment zones to improve opportunities in the poorest areas
- lifelong learning
- equal opportunities for the disabled and older people
- pension reform
- tackling crime
- improving access to services including cultural and leisure
- a National Strategy for Neighbourhood Renewal
- Information Technology Learning Centres

Further reading:
Geddes, Mike (2000) Social exclusion – new language, new challenges for local authorities. *Public Money and Management* 20(2) 55-60
Reeves, R. and Wintour, P. (1999) The poverty gap: help the poor? Well we'll have to find them first. *The Observer* 19.9.99 18

Department of Health (1999) *Caring about carers: a national strategy for carers.* London: H.M. Government

Summary:
- one in eight people are informal carers

- 855,000 of these care for more than 50 hours per week
- three fifths recieve no visitor support services
- arrangements for meeting their needs are inconsistent and patchy

To improve the lives of informal carers, the paper outlines a package of measures that include:

- improved access to information and a charter outlining standards of service in long-term care
- improving carer involvement in service planning and provision
- protecting carers so that they can work and take breaks
- financial measures such as a second pension for carers; reducing council tax for disabled people; support for neighbourhood services

The document includes a chapter on the protection of young carers and appendixes with helplines and a code of good practice for service providers.

Further reading:
Nolan, Mike (1999) National strategy for carers: the way forward? *British Journal of Nursing* 8(4) 194

Care Standards Act 2000: chapter 14. London: The Stationery Office

Summary: this Act comes into force in April 2002 and pulls together proposals and recommendations for social services in England and Wales taken from recent reports such as *Modernising social services (1998)*. The aim is to regulate:

- children's homes
- care homes
- residential family centres
- independent hospitals and clinics
- nurse agencies
- independent medical agencies
- voluntary adoption agencies

The key provisions include:

- setting up a National Care Standards Commission (with equivalent bodies in Wales, Scotland and Northern Ireland), to regulate care and care homes, children's homes and other independent, private and voluntary agencies
- social care workers (defined as "a person engaged in the provision of personal care for any person") to register with new independent Councils such as the GSCC (and equivalent bodies in Wales, Scotland and Northern Ireland see *Accountable care: the new GSCC (1999)*). These will also regulate the training and education of social workers and set standards for social work using codes of conduct and practice amongst other things
- reforms the regulation of child minding and day care provision, transferring responsibility from local authorities to a new arm of Ofsted. New, national standards will require those wishing to work or come into contact with older children will have to demonstrate their suitability to do so

- Secretary of State to maintain a list of those considered unsuitable for work with vulnerable adults, the list to operate in a similar way to that established under the *Protection of Children Act 1999: chapter14*

Further reading:
Nazarko, L. (2001) A new broom: the Care Standards Act. *Nursing Management* 7(8) 6-9

O'Neale, V. (2000) *Excellence not excuses: inspection of services for ethnic minority children and families.* London: The Stationery Office

Summary: published in the wake of the Stephen Lawrence inquiry, this report looks into issues significant to ethnic minority families, and aims to help local councils improve their awareness and improve their services to such families. The report recognises that personal and institutional racism, immigration, separated families and nationality laws can create particular problems for ethnic minorities. It finds that although intentions are good, most local councils do not have appropriate strategies for delivering quality services (although there are exceptions) and such services that are offered are not sensitive to the needs of ethnic minorities. In addition the report finds that not enough consideration is given to equal opportunities and the specific needs and problems of ethnic minority staff working in social services.

Further reading:
Home Office (1999) *The Stephen Lawrence Inquiry (cm 4262-I).*(William Macpherson) London: The Stationery Office

Gordon, David et al (2000) *Poverty and social exclusion in Britain.* London: Joseph Rowntree Foundation

Summary: this report represents the first findings of the most comprehensive study of poverty in this country. Poverty is measured in terms of "deprivation from goods, services and activities which the majority...defines as being...necessities". It also considers ways of measuring social exclusion. The report begins by noting the Government's commitment to ending poverty - child poverty in 20 years - and in the subsequent chapters looks at: adult poverty, child poverty and the growth of poverty and social exclusion. Lack of paid work as well as insufficient child benefit and dependency allowances are seen as the chief causes of poverty and social exclusion with poverty at the root of the majority of social problems.

Further reading:
Benn, Melissa (2000) It just can't be done. *Community Care* 12.10.2000 14
Brittain, Samuel (2000) The poor need not always be with us. *Search* (33) 8-11
Frean, A. (2000) Quarter of households now living in poverty. *The Times* 11.9.2000 10
Green, Roger (2000) Applying a community needs profiling approach to tackling service user poverty. *British Journal of Social Work* 30(3) 287-303
Maltby, Tony and Walker, Alan (1997) Poverty and social exclusion. *Working with Older People* 1(2) 11-15
Norton, Cherry (2000) One-sixth of Britain's children living below the poverty line. *Independent* 11.9.2000

Office for National Statistics (2000) *Social inequalities 2000 edition.* London: The Stationery Office

Summary: an official report that looks at poverty and for the first time, social exclusion. The difficulties defining terms are discussed: poverty being described in "relation to average standards of living" and social exclusion encompassing "notions of participation in society". The data is based on snapshots of the population with some information relating to change in society. There is data on four main headings:

- people and places: population growth and distribution, age and ethnic status. Information about mortgages, housing and car ownership are related to social status
- income and wealth: distribution of wealth according to age, social and ethnic status, gender and lone parenthood
- education, training and skills: gender differences in educational achievement; the relationship between jobs and skills requirements
- work: this looks at full and part-time work, noting gender, age and ethnic differences

Further reading:
Travis, Alan (2000) How gap between rich and poor has grown. *The Guardian* 11.5.2000 8

Audit Commission (2001) *Change here!: managing change to improve local services.* London: Audit Commission

Summary: this is aimed at all public service managers in the light of all the reforms instigated by the Labour Government since coming to office in 1997. For change to be "owned", the guide emphasises the need for all change programmes to be user/client focused and tailored to local circumstances. The responsibilities for Government, service staff and in particular, service leaders are indicated and there is a discussion of the various merits of four types of organisational change namely: *surgery* and *transformation* ('step' changes) and *operational gains* and *evolutionary learning* ('incremental' change).

Further reading:
Iles, Valerie and Sutherland, Kim 'Organisational change: a review for healthcare managers, professionals and researchers. [WWW] http://www.lshtm.ac.uk/php/hsru/sdo/whatsnew.htm (11.02.02)

Henwood, Melanie (2001) *Future imperfect? Report of the King's Fund Care and Support Inquiry.* London: King's Fund

Summary: the Inquiry was set up to examine care and support for the 2 million adults in Britain needing care. The method involved taking written submissions, holding discussions and consultative meetings with service users and carers. On the one hand the Inquiry found a commitment to providing a quality service, with many examples of good practice. On the other hand, inadequate funding and bearing the brunt of negative criticism has lead to low morale. Directed at the GSCC, the Department of Health, the Department of Education and Training, trusts, the Learning and Skills Council and local authorities, the Inquiry's recommendations arise from the following issues:

- a conflict between promoting quality and not enough funding, even to keep the service "standing still"
- underdeveloped skills and knowledge from a traditionally unskilled workforce
- problems with recruitment and retention
- inconsistent regulation and staff training
- inadequate management
- the need to involve clients and their carers when receiving and planning services
- historically the care sector suffers from poor image and low status

Jarvis, Sarah (2001) *Skill mix in primary care: implications for the future.* London: Department of Health, Medical Practices Committee

Summary: in spite of an increase in the use of skill mix there is a lack of evidence that skill mix is cost effective, safe or satisfactory for users and providers. The report summarises some of the existing evidence on skill mix eg: in some areas of nursing, skill mix has led to deskilling and reduced morale among staff. The new NHS Workforce Development Confederations have the remit to review workforce development plans in the health economy.

Supplementary Reading

Banks, Penny and Roberts, Emilie (2001) *More breaks for carers?* London: King's Fund

Brooks, Fiona and Gillam, Stephen (2001) *New beginnings – why patient and public involvement in primary care?* London: King's Fund

Carers National Association (1999) *Taking action to support carers.* London: King's Fund

Department of Health (1998) *The new NHS: modern dependable: primary care groups; delivering the agenda.* London: Department of Health

Family Policy Studies Centre (2000) *Family poverty and social exclusion.* London: FPSC

Farrell, Christine et al (1999) *A new era for community care? What people want from health, housing and social care services.* London: King's Fund

Harrison, Anthony (ed) *Health care UK: an annual review of health care policy.* (annual) London: King's Fund

Holzhausen, Emily (1997) *Still battling? The Carers' Act one year on.* London: Carers National Association

Holzhausen, Emily Pearlman, Vicky and Jackson, Annie (2001) *Caring on the breadline: the financial implications of caring.* London: Carers National Association

Howarth, Catherine and Kenway, Peter (1998) *Monitoring poverty and social exclusion: why Britain needs a key indicators report.* London: New Policy Institute

Kohner, Nancy and Hill, Alison P. (2000) *Help! Does my patient know more than me?* London: King's Fund

Lucas, Karen Grosvenor, Tim, and Simpson, Roona (2001) *Transport, the environment and social exclusion.* London: York Publishing Serivces for Joseph Rowntree

Warner, L. and Wexler, S. (1998) *Eight hours a day and taken for granted.* London: Princess Royal Trust for Carers

3 Public Health

Department of Health (1992) *The health of the nation: a strategy for health in England (cm 1986).* London: HMSO

Summary: aim is to secure improvements in the general health of the population of England with the emphasis on disease prevention and health promotion. Aims to add years to life by increasing life expectancy and reducing premature death; and add life to years by increasing years lived free from ill health; reducing and minimising adverse effects of illness and disability; promoting healthy lifestyles and healthy physical and social environments; and improving the quality of life overall. Five key areas selected for action:

- Cancers
- Coronary heart disease and stroke
- Mental illness
- HIV/AIDS and sexual health
- Accidents

Each key area has overall objectives for improved health and specific targets to be met with emphasis placed on risk factors e.g. smoking.

Recognises that targets cannot be met by NHS alone and advocates development of "healthy alliances" between organisations such as local authorities and health authorities and individuals to work together to improve health.

Sets out how the strategy will be monitored, reviewed and developed.

Further reading:
Calman, Kenneth (1993) Challenges in the Health of the nation. *Health Education Journal* 52(3) 183
George, M. (1992) The health of the nation. *Nursing Standard* 6(44) 18-9
Health Visitors' Association (1991) "The health of the nation": the HVA responds. *Health Visitor* 64(11) 365-7
Lawrence, Martin (1992) Caring for the future. *British Medical Journal* 305(6850) 400-2
Whitty, Paula and Jones, Ian (1992) Public health heresy: a challenge to the puchasing orthodoxy. *British Medical Journal* 6833(304) 1039-41

Department of Health (1993) *Targeting practice: the contribution of nurses, midwives and health visitors.* London: Department of Health

Summary: document aims to encourage understanding of the contribution nurses, midwives and health visitors have made to *The health of the nation (1992)* through the dissemination of current good practice. Gives examples of good practice in each of the five key areas. The principles of good practice and advice on how to use them are outlined. It suggests ways practice might be improved. Emphasises need for evaluation of practice and the use of evidence-based practice.

Department of Health and NHS Executive (1994) *Public health in England: roles and responsibilities of the Department of Health and the NHS.* London: HMSO

Summary: outlines major public health functions and sets out the future public health roles and responsibilities within the Department of Health, the NHS Executive and the NHS. Emphasises that protecting, promoting and improving the public health in England is one of the key responsibilities of the Secretary of State for Health, and with the implementation of *The health of the nation (1992)*, there is a need for a pan-government approach to health.

First section of the report looks at the roles and public health responsibilities of various departments e.g. NHS Executive, and the management of public health.

Annex A and B set out in more detail the future roles and responsibilities of the Public Health Group and the International Relations Group in the Department of Health, the NHS Executive and the new health authorities.

Further reading:
Cernik, K. and Wearne, M. (1994) Promoting the integration of primary care and public health. *Nursing Times* 90(43) 44-5
Harris, A. and Shapiro, J. (1994) Purchasers, professionals and public health: a need for a more radical appraisal of roles. *British Medical Journal* 308(6926) 426-7

Department of Health Standing Nursing and Midwifery Advisory Committee (1995) *Making it happen: public health: the contribution, role and development of nurses, midwives and health visitors: report of the Standing Nursing and Midwifery Advisory Committee.* London: HMSO

Summary: emphasises the importance of public health as a collective way of working to improve the health and well-being of people. Identifies the major contribution that nursing, midwifery and health visiting are making to public health and that they are fundamental in promoting health in local communities. The report makes recommendations for policy, education, research and development and organisational frameworks to ensure this is developed. The majority of recommendations are for purchasers in commissioning primary and secondary care, areas for further research and for other national bodies particularly with regard to nursing, midwifery and health visiting education. Gives examples of existing good practice to build on.

Department of Health (1998) *Our healthier nation: a contract for health (cm 3852).* London: The Stationery Office

Summary: consultative document on public health with two key aims:
1. 'Improve the health of the population as a whole by increasing the length of people's lives and the number of years people spend free from illness'.
2. 'Improve the health of the worst off in society and to narrow the health gap'.

To achieve these two aims the Government proposes a 'national contract for better health' in which government, local communities and individuals will work together to improve health. The Government proposals include working internationally to improve health, ensuring that all national policies take full account of health, informing the public of health risks and the information they require to improve their health.

Health Authorities will have a key role in the development of local Health Improvement Programmes and will be expected to work closely with local authorities, primary care groups and local organisations. Health Action Zones will be set up and a network of Healthy Living Centres will be developed.

The government identifies four key targets to be achieved by 2010:
- heart disease and stroke - reduce the death rate by one-third in people under 65
- accidents - reduce by one-fifth
- cancer - reduce the death rate by one-fifth amongst people under 65
- mental health - reduce the death rate by one-sixth

Further reading:
Allen, D. (1998) Public health for all. *Community Practitioner* 71(3) 12-13
Moore, A. (1998) Target practice. *Nursing Standard* 12 (35) 24-25
Moores, Y. (1998) Nursing the patient better. *Nursing Times* 94(14) 36-37
Peckham, S. (1998) The missing link. *Health Service Journal* 108(5606) 22-23
Pickersgill, F. (1998) Nursing solutions. *Nursing Standard* 12 (42) 26-27

Department of Health (1998) *Independent inquiry into inequalities in health.* (chair Donald Acheson) London: The Stationery Office

Summary: this inquiry was carried out to influence health policy. The report identifies socioeconomic factors and lifestyle as crucial to health well-being. Some of the key areas include poverty, unemployment, housing, nutrition, families, ethnic and gender inequalities and disability. There are 39 recommendations listed at the end, many of which have implications for government policy. It is suggested that policies on education, employment, social services and other areas are constantly assessed and improved with health in mind. The last three of these relate to some of the areas covered in *The New NHS: modern, dependable (1998)* and *Our healthier nation (1998)* about equity of access and services and cooperation between health and social services.

Further reading:
Allen, D. (1999) Back in the Black. *Community Practitioner* 72(2) 11-12
Townsend, Peter and Davidson, Nick (1982) *Inequalities in health: the Black report.* (chair Douglas Black). Harmondsworth: Penguin

Department of Health (1999) *Saving lives: our healthier nation (cm 4386).* London: The Stationery Office

Summary: a white paper that grew out of *Our healthier nation (1998)* and *Independent inquiry into inequalities in health (1998).* An action plan with responsibilities for the public, community care services and Government that sets targets to reduce death rates in cancer, heart disease, stroke, accidents and mental health to be achieved by the year 2010, saving 300,000 lives. As well as a commitment to the proposals made in *Our healthier nation (1998)*, initiatives include:
- 'health skills' and 'expert patient' programmes to help people manage their health and illnesses

- tackling poverty and unemployment
- tackling smoking, sexual health, food safety, drugs and alcohol use, fluoridation and communicable diseases
- improving public health through a health development agency and a public health development fund

Further reading:
Crail, Mark (1999) Watching expiry dates. *Health Service Journal* 109(5663) 9-11

National Audit Office (2001) *Tackling obesity in England: report by the Comptroller and Auditor General.* London: The Stationery Office

Summary: since 1980, obesity has trebled in England and has serious implications in terms of contributing to disease, premature mortality and considerable financial consequences for the NHS. Findings:

- over half the women of this country and two thirds of men are either overweight or obese
- obesity can lead to: heart disease, type-2 diabetes, high blood pressure and osteoarthritis
- estimated cost to the NHS: £1/2 billion a year
- the main reason for the increase is a combination of less active lifestyles and changes in eating patterns: an excess of energy intake over expenditure

Because this is a lifestyle issue, there are limited ways for policy to affect changes, however recommendations include:

- cross-government initiatives in the areas of education, physical activity and diet, largely targeted at school children
- NICE and the Department of Health need to develop guidelines for the management of overweight and obese patients in primary care – the report gives an initial guide for general practitioners
- Health Authorities to develop Health Improvement Programmes that involve partner agencies in schemes to increase physical activity and improve diet
- an appendix lists 19 policies and initiatives that address the problem of obesity

Further reading:
Wardle, J. and Griffith, J. (2001) Socioeconomic status and weight control practices in British adults. *Journal of Epidemiology and Community Health* 55(3) 185-190
World Health Organisation (2000) *Obesity: preventing and managing the world epidemic: report of a WHO consultation.* Geneva: WHO

House of Commons Health Committee (2001) *Second report: public health (session 2000-1): HC30-I and HC30-II.* London: The Stationery Office

Summary: the Committee's brief was to look at how well the Trusts, Health Authorities and the Government were coordinated in delivering public health, looking in particular at agencies such as Health Action Zones, Health Improvement Programmes and Healthy Living Centres. As well as taking evidence, the Committee visited Cuba who achieves good health outcomes and a high life expectancy in spite of poor resources and trade restrictions. Findings include:

- public health is underfunded and has a low profile
- the momentum gathered from *Saving lives (1997)* has largely dissipated: too much emphasis is placed on acute curative care, with waiting lists the only mark of effectiveness
- stronger leadership is needed and stronger partnerships for a broad-based approach to public health
- public health should be seen as an applied science, using knowledge to bring about change, not just gathering information for its own sake
- agencies should avoid constant reorganisation; consider creating incentives; build up the research base and learn from past experience
- Chief Medical Officer to publish report as a matter of urgency (see below)

Further reading:
Coote, Anna (2001) Vanishing act. *Community Care* 14.6.2001 22
Department of Health (2001) *Government response to the House of Commons Select Committee on Health's second report on public health (cm 5242).* London: HMSO
Hunter, David and Goodwin, Neil (2001) How to get promoted. *Health Service Journal* 111(5764) 26-7

Department of Health (2001) *The report of the Chief Medical Officer's project to strengthen the public health function.* London: Department of Health

Summary: long overdue report with extensive recommendations that include:
- improve public awareness, health surveillance and the evidence base
- improve coordination, establish a Public Health Forum and strengthen existing networks
- "joined up working": share public health information and expertise at local and regional level; raise the profile of the Director of Public Health's annual report; promote flexible working between agencies
- promote sustainable community development with full public involvement
- public health workforce: to increase, to be multidisciplinary and adequately funded; within the workforce, strengthen leadership and proactive working and develop plans for education and training

Department of Health (2001) *National strategy for sexual health and HIV.* London: Department of Health

Summary: the variations in levels of sexual health services as well as an increase in the prevalence of sexually transmitted infections (STI's) have led to this strategy. The strategy is a ten-year commitment with fourteen proposals designed to raise the level of services and reduce the incidence of STI's, HIV and unwanted pregnancies. These proposals include:
- pilots of one-stop clinics
- primary care youth services
- screening for chlamydia and routine HIV testing in genitourinary medicine clinics

- ensuring parity in abortion services
- making contraceptive services available as well as hepatitis B vaccine

Chief Medical Officer (2002) *Getting ahead of the curve: a strategy for combating infectious diseases (including other aspects of health protection).* London: Department of Health

Summary: this fulfills one of the pledges of *Saving lives: our healthier nation (1999)* and takes in protection against chemical and radiological hazards.

The present global situation: HIV/AIDS, malaria and T.B. account for millions of deaths each year, and experts agree that the threat of an influenza pandemic such as occurred after the First World War is not a question of 'whether', but 'when'. Risk of infection is increased by world travel, microorganisms becoming more virulent and resistant to treatment, more people with compromised immunity and changes in the way we use land and the environment. In England, hospital-acquired infections may account for as many as 5,000 deaths while numbers diagnosed with HIV will rise to 29,000 by 2003. The document also notes the impact of crises due to BSE/vCJD, meningitis, influenza, bronchitis and e coli.

Causes: new diseases, animal-transmitted diseases, poor hygiene, below-standard medical practice and unpredictable situations such as the release of anthrax in the USA in 2001.

Proposals include:
- to establish new agencies (especially since the abolition of health authorities) for the surveillance, control and prevention of infectious diseases at national, regional and local levels – the National Infection Control Protection Agency, local health protection services and a national expert panel
- to improve systems of surveillance
- new action plans to establish priorities with: T.B., hospital-acquired infections, blood-borne and sexually transmitted diseases
- to appoint an Inspector of Microbiology along with an improved microbiology laboratory service
- to establish a plan to combat the threat of deliberate release of toxic agents
- improve public information, staff development and training, research and development and to review the law

Supplementary reading:

Ballinger, Steve (2002) *Home sick: Shelter and Bradford & Bingley's campaign for healthy homes.* London: SHELTER

Department of Health (2001) *From vision to reality.* London: Department of Health

Department of Health (1998) *Health improvement programmes: planning for better health and better health care.* London: The Department of Health

Department of Health *On the state of the public health: the annual report of the Chief Medical Officer of the Department of Health.* (annual) London: The Stationery Office

4 Quality, Accountability and Patient Rights

Parker, Roy (1990) *Safeguarding standards: a report on the desirability and feasibility of establishing a UK independent body to regulate and promote good practice in social work and social care.* London: National Institute for Social Work

Summary: a steering committee was set up in 1987 to consider establishing an independent body to regulate social work and social care: General Social Services Council - GSSC. The Joseph Rowntree Memorial Trust funded this feasibility study following a report in 1982 that had judged the implementation of such a council as "premature". Changes in social services during the 80's strengthened the case for an independent council whereas there was no increase in the arguments against it.

Department of Health (1991) *The patient's charter.* London HMSO

Summary: this launched the Conservative goverment's Citizen's Charter initiative in the specific area of the NHS and its standards. The introduction stresses the importance of maintaining the tenets on which the NHS was originally founded, i.e. that it is freely available to all at the point of need. The basic message is 'the patient comes first'. It invites views and suggestions from patients and also imposes an obligation on health authorities to provide information about its services. The three main sections are:

- existing patients' rights, i.e. access to health records and emergency care
- three new rights: information on local services and standards; guaranteed maximum two-year waiting lists; full investigation and response to complaints
- nine national charter standards such as: respect for religious beliefs; minimum waiting times for ambulances; assessment in accident and emergency departments and the introduction of the "named nurse" concept

Further reading:
Brown, Colin (1991) Do as you would be done by. *Health Service Journal* 101(5268) 8
Cohen, P. (1994) Passing the buck?...Patient's charter seems to have raised the expectations of people using the health service. *Nursing Times* 90(13) 28-30
Shuttleworth, A. (1992) Will the charter work? Readers views on the Patient's charter. *Professional Nurse* 7(7) 439-41
Stocking, Barbara (1991) Patients' charter. *British Medical Journal* 303(6811) 1148-9

Department of Health (1995) *The patient's charter and you.* London: Department of Health

Summary: expanded and updated edition of the *Patient's charter (1991)*. Sets out patients' rights and standards of service they can expect to receive. Distinguishes between rights which all patients will receive all the time and expectations which are standards of service which the NHS is aiming to achieve. Areas included are:

- rights and standards throughout the NHS e.g. access to services
- GP services e.g. registering with and changing doctors
- hospital services e.g. reducing waiting times
- community services e.g. appointment times
- ambulance services e.g. ambulance arrival times
- dental, optical and pharmaceutical services
- outlines how patients can help the NHS by using its services responsibly e.g. by returning equipment

Further reading:
Friend, B. (1995) Shallow standards: pressure to meet Patient's charter targets means that some hospitals are fiddling the figures. *Nursing Times* 91(28) 14-5
Ryland, R.K. (1996) The Patients' charter: the United Kingdom experience. *Journal of Advanced Nursing* 23(6) 1059-60
Farrell, Christine (1998) *The patient's charter: past and future.* London: King's Fund

Harding, Tessa and Beresford, Peter (1996) *The standards we expect: what service users and carers want from social services workers.* London: National Institute for Social Work

Summary: this report forms part of a study on standards commissioned by the Department of Health. The people involved represented a wide cross-section of voluntary and user-controlled organisations across the country and welcomed the opportunity to contribute to setting standards of practice. The main points are:

- making involvement possible, including a more 'child-friendly' forum that would enable children to voice their needs in a less daunting setting
- making standards stick – across the board standards were viewed as inconsistent. Standards should not merely exist on paper but be enforceable in practice. Monitoring and improving standards should be ongoing with people called to account if they do not meet the standards
- making standards consistent – common standards should be applied across health and social services and also across children's services and education

The final report falls into four parts covering the quality of relationships; the quality of skills; the quality of services and areas for improvement with plans for action.

Caldicott Committee: Department of Health (1997) *Report on the review of patient identifiable information.* (chair Fiona Caldicott) London: Department of Health

Summary: the review was commissioned because of the development of information technology that has allowed patient information to be disseminated widely and quickly. The sixteen recommendations include:

- to strengthen the awareness of the need for confidentiality and security
- organisations to appoint guardians responsible for safeguarding confidentiality
- there must be protocols written about the exchange of information and access to patient identity

- a NHS number to replace all other identifiers as soon as possible
- health and information systems to incorporate best principles at the design stage
- GP claims and payments to avoid transmission of patients' details

Further reading:
Barber, Barry (1998) How should we treat personal medical data. *British Journal of Healthcare Computing and Information Management* 15(1) 23-26
Walker, Phil (1998) Caldicott implementation: protecting and using confidential patient information in the modern NHS. *British Journal of Healthcare Computing and Information Management* 15(7) 28-30
Wells, Mike (1998) Caldicott guardians and the NHS strategic tracing service. *British Journal of Healthcare Computing and Information Management* 15(7) 32-35

Department of Health (1998) *A first class service: quality in the new NHS*. London: Department of Health

Summary: consultation document focusing on improving quality standards, efficiency, openness and accountability. The Government proposes:

- a National Institute for Clinical Excellence (NICE) which will assess new and existing interventions for their clinical- and cost-effectiveness and produce national guidance for clinicians and patients
- National Service Frameworks which will lay down the care that different groups of patients can expect to receive in major care areas or disease groups

These quality standards will be applied locally through a system of clinical governance, extended life-long learning and professional self-regulation. Standards will be monitored through three new mechanisms:

- a Commission for Health Improvement
- a National Framework for Assessing Performance
- an annual National Survey of Patient and User Experience

Further reading:
Crinson, Iain (1999) Clinical governance: the new NHS, new responsibilities. *British Journal of Nursing* 8(7) 449-53
Editorial (1998) First class only. *Nursing Standard* 12 (43) 12-14
Pickersgill, F. (1998) Raising the standards. *Nursing Standard* 12 (44) 22-3
Walshe, K. (1998) Going first class with the NHS. *Health Service Journal* 108(5612) 18-19

NHS Executive (1998) *In the public interest: developing a strategy for public participation in the NHS*. London: The Stationery Office

Summary: this report looks at the public's involvement in decision-making for health provision in the new NHS and in the light of greater access to information generally. The rationale and ethical considerations for public participation are discussed in the first two sections. Four models of participation are outlined in the third and fourth sections:

- direct participation of users
- informed view of citizens

- community development
- local scrutiny and accountability

The final section gives recommendations for health policy in relation to NHS staff such as improved dissemination of information, the role of primary care groups and partnerships with other agencies.

Further reading:
Ainsworth, Steve (1998) Voices of dissent. *Health Service Journal* 108(5618) 23

Public Interest Disclosure Act 1998: chapter 23. London: The Stationery Office

Summary: this came into force in 1999 as an addition to the *Employment Rights Act 1996*. The Act is designed to protect from victimisation individuals who speak out (or "whistleblow") in the interests of public safety.

1. the meanings and circumstances surrounding disclosure are made clear, for instance disclosure does not qualify if it involves an individual breaking the law or if it is made purely for personal gain
2. employees may bring a complaint to an Employment Tribunal and be compensated for unfair dismissal, redundancy or any other kind of victimisation
3. "gagging" clauses in contracts and severance agreements will be void

    Health Service Circular 1999/198 outlines how the Act will apply to the NHS; organisations are advised to write local whistleblowing policies.

Further reading:
Employment Rights Act 1996: chapter 18. London: The Stationery Office
Snell, J. (1998) Blowing in the wind. *Health Service Journal* 108(5619) 20-23
Taylor, H. / NHSE (1999) *The Public Interest Disclosure Act 1998: whistleblowing in the NHS.* (HSC 1999/198) Leeds: Department of Health
Vickers, L. (1999) Freedom of speech in the National Health Service. *Journal of Social Welfare and Family Law* 21(2) 121-134

Human Rights Act 1998: chapter 42. London: The Stationery Office

Summary: this came into force in October 2000 and brings the *European Convention on Human Rights (1999)* into UK law. The articles are:
- right to life
- prohibition of torture
- prohibition of slavery and forced labour
- right to liberty and security
- right to a fair trial
- no punishment without law
- right to respect for private and family life
- freedom of thought, conscience and religion
- freedom of expression

- freedom of assembly and association
- right to marry
- prohibition of discrimination
- prohibition of abuse of rights

Protocols are later additions to the original convention. They are:
- protection of property
- right to education
- right to free elections
- abolition of the death penalty

Further reading:
British Medical Association (2000) *The medical profession and human rights: handbook for a changing agenda.* London: Zed Books
Council of Europe (1999) *European Convention on Human Rights and Property Rights.* Strasbourg: Council of Europe/Conseil de l'Europe
International Council of Nurses (1999) *ICN on health and human rights.* Geneva: ICN
United Nations (1998) *Universal declaration of human rights.* Geneva: UN
Wilkinson, R. and Caulfield, Helen (2000) *The Human Rights Act: a practical guide for nurses.* London: Whurr

Department of the Environment, Transport and the Regions, and Department of Health (1999) *Better care, higher standards: a charter for long term care.* London: The Stationery Office

Summary: designed to encourage the cooperation of local health, housing and social services, in order to help users of long term care, and to improve services to them. The Charter is aimed at anyone over eighteen with long term care needs, and their carers. It sets standards for the services provided by local health, housing and social service departments. These standards are published in local charters that should be widely available from June 2000; information is also given about what to do when services fall below the standard. The six main areas are:

- providing information to users and carers about the services available
- understanding and responding to the needs of users and carers
- finding suitable living accommodation
- promoting and helping with independent living
- receiving appropriate health care
- assisting carers

The Charter will help to ensure consistency across the country: elements of the charter are already in place in some areas, but not all. Finally, users and carers are reminded that they also have a part to play in achieving good outcomes; the Charter encourages them to:

- give full information
- keep appointments
- keep service providers up-to-date with their needs

- follow medical advice about treatment and medication
- look after equipment
- tell service providers what they might do to improve their services

Department of Health (1999) *Supporting doctors, protecting patients: a consultation paper on preventing, recognising and dealing with poor clinical performance of doctors in the NHS in England.* London: Department of Health

Summary: a paper that arises from *A first class service (1998)* and the recent inquiries into medical malpractice. The common themes are: a pattern of poor practice over a long period; problems known about but not officially; the failure of systems that were set up to detect problems. Proposals include:
- improving professional self-regulation and accountability
- the clinical governance programme to ensure a thorough review of quality
- measures involving education, supervision and stress relief to prevent problems occurring in the first place

For handling and dealing with problems, three steps are identified:
1. identifying which category it falls into i.e.: personal misconduct, serious mistake or others' concerns about clinical performance
2. setting up Assessment and Support Centres around the country
3. employer or health authority to take responsibility for carrying out the findings of the Assessment and Support Centres; Health Authorities to have the power to suspend GPs.

Further reading:
Chief Medical Officer (2001) *Harold Shipman's clinical practice, 1974 – 1998.* (chair Richard Baker) London: The Stationery Office
Department of Health (2000) *An inquiry into quality and practice within the NHS arising from the actions of Rodney Ledward: the report.* (chair Jean Ritchie) London: Department of Health
Hill, A.P. and Baeza, Juan (1999) Dealing with things that go wrong.
Lancet 354(9196) 2099-10
Hutchinson, Martin (2000) Will regulation reforms help doctors improve?
Hospital Doctor 20.1.00 30-33
Jewell, D. (2000) Supporting doctors, or the beginning of the end for self-regulation?
British Journal of General Practice 50(450) 4-5

Brand, Don (1999) *Accountable care: developing the General Social Care Council.* London: Joseph Rowntree Foundation

Summary: this describes how the notion of standard setting in social care evolved since 1990 with a General Social Care Council (GSCC) proposed in 1993. Comparing the councils in England, Scotland and Wales, the main principles that emerge are to do with empowering and protecting users, with a strong user representation and "open" working. A survey of user organisations reveals a confidence in the GSCC provided it is fully responsive to users and not remote or bureaucratic. Staff contracts will include codes of conduct and staff are content with this provided there is strong support and access to training. On the other hand, employers must have defined expectations in recruitment, supervision and management and there must be a code of practice for handling complaints and disciplinaries.

Further reading:
Department of Health (1996) *Obligations of care: a consultation paper on the setting of conduct and practice standards for social services staff.* London: Department of Health
Harding, Tessa and Beresford, Peter (1996) *Standards we expect: what service users and carers want from social services departments.* London: National Institute for Social Work
Parker, R.A. (1990) *Safeguarding standards.* London: National Institute for Social Work

Department of Health (2000) *A quality strategy for social care.* London: The Stationery Office

Summary: the strategy builds on *Modernising social services (1998)*; it outlines the reforms required in working practices and the training and managment needed to improve the quality of social services. Across the country, social services should:

- promote independence
- strengthen families by supporting parental responsibility
- improve the life chances of children in need
- tackle inequality and social exclusion

There are too many failings in the system however, due to bureaucracy, inflexibility, poor coordination, inadequately trained staff, and inconsistent service delivery from one area to another. The aims of the strategy therefore are to:

- tackle inconsistency
- create a new Social Care Institute for Excellence to convert evidence-based knowledge into quality practice
- introduce a new Quality Framework to help local councils improve the quality of their social care service
- improve workforce training at all levels from management down

Further reading:
Editorial (2001) Raising the standard of social care in England. *Professional Social Work* January 2001 6-7
Statham, D. (2000) Look and learn. *Community Care* 5.10.01 24

Department of Health (2000) *An organisation with a memory: report of an expert group on learning from adverse events in the NHS.* (chair Liam Donaldson) London: The Stationery Office

Summary: the report claims the NHS often fails to learn from adverse events and has an old fashioned approach when compared with other sectors. A fundamental review would provide many benefits in terms of saving lives, preventing harm and freeing up much needed resources. To this end the report recommends:

- a unified mechanism for report and analysis when things go wrong
- a more open working culture so as to encourage the reporting of errors
- a mechanism for making sure that recommended changes are put into practice
- a wider appreciation of the 'value system' approach to learning from errors

Further reading:
Barach, Paul and Small, Stephen D. (2000) How the NHS can improve safety and learning by learning free lessons from near misses.
British Medical Journal 320(7251) 1683-4
Scott, Helen (2000) Individuals must not take the blame for the system.
British Journal of Nursing 9(12) 744
Sommerville, Fiona (2000) Systems fail, not just individuals. *Nursing Standard* 96(32) 23
Snell, Jane (2000) The errors of our ways. *Health Management* 4(7) 14-5

Department of Health (2000) *Your guide to the NHS.*
London: Department of Health

Summary: published after *The NHS plan (2000)*, this is – in all but name – a third edition of *The patients' charter 1991*. It sets out what patients may expect from the NHS as well as what is promised over the next five years.

- begins by stating the ten core principles of the NHS including that it should be free to all at the point of need and that it aims to be needs-led, seamless and working to a consistently high standard
- lists patients' responsibilities to themselves – including tips for healthy living – and to the service
- explains the functions of the different agencies such as NHS Direct, general practitioners, pharmacists etc

Planned improvements include:
- further development of NHS Direct
- promises to do with waiting times and cancellations
- improvements in the standard of hygiene and quality of meals
- greater patient representation and involvement in the planning of services

Chief Medical Officer (2001) *Harold Shipman's clinical practice 1974 – 1998.* (chair Richard Baker) London: The Stationery Office

Summary: this report takes pains to stress that it is an audit of Harold Shipman's clinical practice, not a full inquiry. It does not concern itself with why things happened or with the testimony of witnesses, nor does it attempt to establish cause of death of any of his patients. Looking at medical certificates of cause of death (MCCDs) issued by Shipman, cremation forms issued, the deaths of all Shipman's patients and his practice in prescribing controlled drugs, the audit is looking for patterns of death by age group, gender, place and time of day and the connexions between death and patient history.
Findings:
- Harold Shipman issued 499 MCCDs whilst working in Hyde compared with a maximum of 210 issued by any of the other six local GPs

- there was an unusually high number deaths at home, among females over sixty five
- deaths occurred in the afternoon, with Shipman present, giving cause of death as heart disease, stroke or old age
- this pattern is evident from his first years of practice
- the connexion between cause of death and patient history appears tenuous
- the audit trail as to prescribing controlled drugs is unclear
- Shipman's record-keeping was poor

Recommendations include:
- the monitoring of general practitioners to be reviewed so as to include death rates, prescribing controlled drugs and record keeping
- a system is needed to gather information on numbers of deaths and MCCDs issued
- MCCDs must include a brief record of cause and circumstances of death as well as a brief patient history
- GP validation should include assessment of record-keeping
- the storage of clinical records must be reviewed
- GP's controlled drugs register should be open to inspection
- patient records and GP's and pharmacists' controlled drugs registers should note batch numbers

Further reading:
Carey, Penny (2001) Getting away with it. *Health Care Risk Report* 7(6) 20-1
Caverford, Cathy (2001) Spectre of Shipman still haunts GPs. *Doctor* 8.2.2001 40-42
Pritchard, Lisa (2001) Hyde and seek. *BMA News* 12.5.2001 12-14
Ramsay, Sarah (2001) Audit further exposes UK's worst serial killer. *The Lancet* 357(9250) 123-4

Department of Health (2001) *Reference guide to consent for examination or treatment.* London: Department of Health

Summary: a guide for health professionals on the law surrounding valid consent. Guidance is given on: seeking consent; when consent is withdrawn or refused; gaining consent from "adults without capacity" as well as children and young people; withdrawing and withholding life-prolonging treatment. Issues raised by the *Human Rights Act 1998* are considered along with removal of organs from persons declared dead.

Further reading:
Austin, Julie (2001) Whose life is it anyway? Or self-determination and the capacity to give consent to treatment. *Health Service Manager Briefing* 2001 (64) 6-8
Billcliff, N. McCabe, E. and Brown, K.W. (2001) Informed consent to medication in long-term psychiatric in-patients. *Psychiatric Bulletin* 25(4) whole issue
British Medical Association (2001) *Consent, rights and choices in health care for children and young people.* London: BMJ Books
Royal College of General Practitioners and Royal College of Physicians (2001) Medical treatment at the end of life: a position statement. *Clinical Medicine* 2001 1(2) 115-117

Bristol Royal Infirmary Inquiry (2001) *The report of the public inquiry into children's heart surgery at the Bristol Royal Infirmary 1984-1995: learning from Bristol (cm5207).* (chair Ian Kennedy)
London: The Stationery Office

Summary: at £15m this is the longest, most comprehensive public inquiry ever held on the NHS. It follows a General Medical Council inquiry into the performance of three consultants: Wisheart, Dhasmana and Roylance following allegations of malpractice made by consultant anaesthetist Stephen Bolsin in 1995. Bolsin implied that fear of losing funding had caused the unit to 'turn a blind eye' to the unacceptable mortality rates. That inquiry looked at complex heart operations on fifty three children of whom twenty nine died and and four were left brain-damaged. Wisheart and Roylance were struck off, Dhasmana was sacked and barred from operating on children for three years. This Inquiry's brief was:

- to look into the care and management of children under one year undergoing complex cardiac surgery at Bristol between the years 1984 and 1995
- to look into the adequacy of the whole service
- to look into what happened when concerns were raised and why they were not addressed

The Inquiry found circumstances and situations that are by no means unique to Bristol and therefore urged that its recommendations be considered by all service areas within the NHS. The 200 recommendations arise from the following issues:

- RESPECT and HONESTY: this refers to the importance of communicating with patients and families, keeping them informed, involving them in decisions of care and providing support in the process of giving consent
- LEADERSHIP: this looks at the roles of the Department of Health, NICE and CHI, the Council for Quality of Healthcare and at local level, the roles of trusts, their consultants, chief executives and senior managers
- COMPETENCE: at all levels of education and training there should be greater emphasis given to 'non-clinical' skills such as communication, reflective practice leadership and teamwork. As well as the regulating bodies (eg the GMC, NMC etc) a Council for the Regulation of Healthcare Professionals with statutory powers should integrate the different systems of professional regulation, promoting common curricula and shared learning
- SAFETY: there should be a national system for reporting events in safety and confidence, and systems for examining "sentinel" events in order to learn from them. Throughout, the Inquiry abhors blaming and scapegoating in favour of open systems of working that can acknowledge mistakes will occur and can be learnt from
- STANDARDS: NICE to be reponsible for coordinating everything related to standard-setting, noting that some standards should be compulsory and others set to be achieved over time. The role of the CHI needs further development as do the mechanisms for monitoring performance at local and national levels
- PUBLIC EMPOWERMENT: this refers to involving the public in commissioning and providing care services at all levels. It urges 'transparent' working practices by the

professional bodies, and that Patient Councils, Patients' Forums and the PCTs' Patient and Advocacy Liaison Service provide for fully involving the wider public – not just existing patients

- CARE OF CHILDREN: this looks at communication with children and their parents; the need for child-centred facilities with specialist trained staff; greater integration of primary, acute and specialist care. The proposed National Service Framework should be published as a matter of urgency and must include mechanisms for setting and reviewing standards. The Inquiry also proposes appointing a National Director for Children's Healthcare Services with consideration given to creating a Children's Commissioner whose role would be to promote the rights of the child in all public areas. There are also specific recommendations to do with care of children with congenital heart disease

Further reading:
Department of Health (2002) *Learning from Bristol: the Department of Health's response to the report of the public inquiry into children's heart surgery at the Bristol Royal Infirmary 1984-1995 (cm5363).* London: The Stationery Office
Walshe, K. and Offen, N. (2001) A very public failure: lessons for quality improvement in healthcare organisations from the Bristol Royal Infirmary.
Quality in Health Care 10(4) 250-56
Health Service Journal (2001) 111 (5764 and 5765) whole issues
Higgins, Joan (2001) The listening blank. *Health Service Journal* 111(5772) 22-25

Department of Health, Department for Education and Employment, Home Office and Chief Medical Officer (2001) *The removal, retention and use of human organs and tissue from post-mortem examination: advice from the CMO.* London: The Stationery Office

Summary: the result of public concern after Bristol and Liverpool parents discovered that their children's organs and tissue had been retained post-mortem without knowledge or consent. There are seventeen recommendations including:

- revision of the law with amendments to ensure that consent is given and pathologists authorised to retain organs
- a code of practice with a standardised consent form and setting standards in good communications
- the appointment of an overseeing Commission of pathology practices
- controls on the import and export of body parts
- a new system of death certification involving an independent medical examiner to address issues raised by the Shipman audit
- bereavement support
- to promote the value of research
- research into less invasive forms of post-mortem examination

Further reading:
Dimond, Bridget (2001) Alder Hey and the retention and storage of body parts. *British Journal of Midwifery* 9(3)

Royal Liverpool Children's Inquiry, House of Commons and Department of Health (2001) *Royal Liverpool Children's Inquiry Report: the Alder Hey report.* (chair Michael Redfern) London: The Stationery Office
Smith, Tom (2001) Push me, pull you. *Health Service Journal* 111(5747) 30-31
Woodcock, Sue (2001) Bodyparts and the law. *Nursing Times* 97(6) 32-34

Staley, Kristina (2001) *Voices, values and health: involving the public in moral decisions.* London: King's Fund

Summary: the result of a debate with Londoners about values and public health. Their views included:

- although final decisions should rest with politicians and professional decision-makers, promoting "collective" health is important
- decision makers should: listen, make final decisions and be ready to justify them publicly
- consultations should be inclusive, without political bias, and they should allow time for thought and discussion, and also review as time passes
- whilst lending legitimacy to decision-making, the danger in public debate is of never reaching a decision
- public debate can allow for accountability, can limit conflict and encourage a collective rather than selfish attitude

Department of Health (2001) *Establishing the new Nursing and Midwifery Council.* London: Department of Health

Summary: this sets out the plan to replace the UKCC and the four national boards with a Nursing and Midwifery Council and a single professional register. Main aims:
- patient welfare paramount
- faster, more "transparent" working procedures
- accountability to the health service and to the public
- the Council to have wider powers to regulate dangerous individuals
- Council to be smaller, elected and with a strong lay representation
- explicit powers to link registration with evidence of professional development

Main changes include:
- a president, first appointed through open competition and then elected by Council
- each member to have a "seconder" to attend meetings and vote in their absence
- a statutory midwifery committee
- wider powers to pay fees and allowances in order to secure the highest possible calibre of membership
- NMC to be accountable to Privy Council instead of the Secretary of State
- Government to have the power set up inquiries into the NMC's performance

Further reading:
Drazek, M (2000) The new Nursing and Midwifery Council: what does modernising mean for midwives. *Practising Midwife* 3(9) 10-2

Duffin, C. (2001) Taking change on board...the metamorphosis of the UKCC to the Nursing and Midwifery Council. *Nursing Standard* 15(23) 12-3

Munro, R. (2001) Clocking in at the council...Nursing and Midwifery Council. *Nursing Times* 97(19) 12-3

Rogers, C and Ryan, C. (2001) Updating regulations with the Nursing and Midwifery Council. *British Journal of Midwifery* 9(5) 268-70

Department of Health (2001) *Building a safer NHS for patients.* London: Department of Health

Summary: a plan to promote patient safety, the key points are:
- standardising the definition and system for reporting adverse events – this leading to an international standard
- a National Patient Safety Agency to collect, analyse and feedback data on adverse events; providing information about safety and producing solutions and national goals
- the system for handling investigations to be either through a Department of Health commission or the Commission for Health Improvement only. Major service failures may lead to a public inquiry led by the Secretary of State for Health
- specific targets include: to reduce to nil the number of patients dying or paralysed by poorly administered spinal injections, to reduce instances of harm in obstetrics and gynaecology and to reduce errors in the use of prescription drugs
- to develop the evidence base on patient safety

Further Reading
Dimond, Bridget (2001) The National Patient Safety Agency. *British Journal of Midwifery* 9(8) 511-4
Lipley, N. (2001) Safe landing. *Nursing Standard* 15(34) 11
MacLeod, Norman (2001) Flying by the seat of our pants. *Nursing Standard* 15(49) 14-15

Department of Health (2001) *Information for social care: a framework for improving quality in social care through better use of information and information technology.* London: The Stationery Office

Summary: information plays a crucial part in the delivery of high quality social care services; sometimes information is the service itself since users need information on available services and Central Government needs information in order to monitor performance of social services. This document provides a "practical toolkit" that councils, the Department of Health and other partner agencies can use to tackle information management. It presents a detailed overview of the main issues i.e.:
- the electronic social care record
- knowledge management
- systems
- access and communication channels
- infrastructure
- culture

- funding
- planning and project management

Supplementary reading:

Commission for Health Improvement (2001) *A guide to clinical governance reviews in NHS acute trusts.* London: Commission for Health Improvement

Data Protection Registrar (1998) *Data Protection Act 1998: an introduction.* Cheshire: Wilmslow

Department of Health (1994) *Being heard: the report of a review committee on NHS complaints procedures.* London: Department of Health

Department of Health (2001) *The essence of care: patient-focused benchmarking for health care practitioners.* London: Department of Health

Department of Health (2001) *Extending choice for patients: a discussion document: proposals for pilot schemes to improve choice and provide faster treatment.* London: Department of Health

Department of Health (2000) *An inquiry into the quality and practice within the NHS arising from the actions of Rodney Ledward.* (chair: Jean Ritchie) London: Department of Health

Department of Health (1999) *Patient and public involvement in the new NHS.* London: Department of Health

Dyke, Greg (1998) *The new NHS charter: a different approach: report on the new NHS charter.* London: Department of Health

General Medical Council 'Maintaining good medical medical practice' [WWW] http://www.gmc-uk.org/standards/MGMP.htm (17.05.02)

National Consumer Council (1999) *Involving users in the delivery of local public services.* London: NCC

National Consumer Council (1999) *Self-regulation of professionals in health care: consumer issues.* London: NCC

NHS (2001) *A commitment to quality, a quest for excellence: a statement on behalf of the Government, the medical profession and the NHS.* London: Department of Health

NHS Executive (1996) *Promoting clinical effectiveness: a framework for action in and through the NHS.* London: NHSE

NHS Executive (1999) *Clinical governance: quality in the new NHS.* London: NHSE

NHS Management Executive (1991) *Framework of audit for nursing services.* London: NHSME

Nursing and Midwifery Council (2002) *Code of professional conduct.* London: NMC

Nursing and Midwifery Council (2002) *Complaints about professional practice.* London: NMC

Nursing and Midwifery council (2002) *Guidelines for records and record-keeping.* London: NMC

Nursing and Midwifery Council (2002) *Guidelines for the administration of medicines.* London: NMC

Royal College of General Practitioners (1999) *Clinical governance: practical advice for primary care in England and Wales.* London: RCGP

Royal College of Nursing (2000) *Clinical Governance: guidance for nurses.* London: RCN

Royal Liverpool Children's Inquiry, House of Commons (2001) *Royal Liverpool Children's Hospital Inquiry report: the Alder Hey report.* (chair Michael Redfern) London: The Stationery Office

UKCC (1996) *Guidelines for professional practice.* London: UKCC

UKCC (2001) *Professional self-regulation and clinical governance.* London: UKCC

5 Education

UKCC (1986) *Project 2000: a new preparation for practice.* London: UKCC

Summary: wide ranging review of the future preparation of nurses, midwives and health visitors for practice. The project team reviews both the current educational patterns and the current and future needs for health care. It presents the case for change and provides a detailed account of the new proposals which are summarised into twenty five recommendations. These include the development of a three year training programme, beginning with a common foundation programme, followed by specialisation into one of four branches, the development of one single level of registered nurse, the cessation of enrolled nurse programmes and the need for student nurses to become supernumerary to the existing NHS staffing establishment.

Further reading:
Robinson, J. (1986) Through the minefield and into the sun? *Senior Nurse* 4(6) 7-9
UKCC (1987) *Project 2000: the final proposals (project paper 9).* London: UKCC

Department of Health (1989) *Working for patients: working paper 10: education and training.* London: HMSO

Summary: forms an integral part of the white paper *Working for patients*. This document deals specifically with the education and training of health care staff in England with the exception of doctors and dentists. The paper proposes fundamental changes in the funding of nurse education, its structure and its organisation.

The document introduces the concept of the purchaser/provider split with the Regional Health Authorities providing direct funding for pre-registration nurse education and nursing colleges and other educational institutions being contracted to provide the courses. Commissioning training will normally be undertaken by a consortia of employers for numbers agreed with the RHAs.

Further reading:
Burke, L.M. (1995) Political principles in action: a critical analysis of education and training: working paper 10 and its implications for nurse education. *Nurse Education Today* 15(5) 381-9

UKCC (1990) *The report of the post-registration education and practice project.* London: UKCC

Summary: in 1989 the UKCC launched a project to develop a framework for education and practice after registration. This discussion paper reports the findings of the project team and proposes, as a result, a series of twelve recommendations. One of the main recommendations is that all practitioners should show they have maintained and developed their professional competence and knowledge through producing a personal professional profile and undertaking a period of study. Other recommendations include a period of support for newly registered practitioners and those returning to nursing after a break of five years or more should complete a return to practice programme.

Further reading:
Green, L (1991) Prepare for PREPP: view from the top. *Nursing Times* 87(8) 24-5
Lauren, C. (1990) A little more PREPP. *Nursing Times* 86(13) 28-30

National Audit Office (1992) *Nursing education: implementation of project 2000 in England.* London: HMSO

Summary: at national level this document details how Project 2000 was introduced, funded and costed with a discussion of the difficulties encountered. At the local level, the NAO examines ten Project 2000 schemes and looks at such issues as recruitment, retention and impact of the new scheme on NHS working practices. The report also looks at the provision of enrolled nurse conversion courses. The NAO finally highlights a number of issues which will need further consideration if this new form of nurse education is to give full value for money.

Further reading:
Elkan, R. and Robinson, J. (1995) Project 2000: a review of published research. *Journal of Advanced Nursing.* 22(2) 386-392
Jowett, S. et al (1994) *Challenges and change in nurse education: a study of the implementation of Project 2000.* Slough: National Foundation for Education Research in England and Wales

UKCC (1994) *The future of professional practice: the Council's standards for education and practice following registration: position statement on policy and implementation March 1994.* London: UKCC

Summary: this document is a detailed account of the UKCC's position on standards for post-registration education and practice. The document outlines the three major requirements, namely:
- standards for a period of support under a preceptor's guidance
- standards for maintaining effective registration
- standards for post-registration education

In each case the UKCC describes how the requirements will be met by the professions, what documents will need to be submitted to the UKCC, the likely implementation periods and which requirements will be statutory. It also details developments in specialist education qualifications and advanced nursing practice.

Further reading:
Cassidy, J. (1994) PREP and you... impact of the final PREP proposals on different members of the profession. *Nursing Times* 90(9) 20-21
Questions and answers...what nurses must do in order to maintain an effective registration. (1995) *Nursing Standard* 9(27 supplement) 7-17
UKCC (1994) *The future of professional practice: the Council's standards for education following registration.* London: UKCC

Hollingworth, Sheila (1997) *Lecturer practitioner roles in England: a report prepared for the Chief Nursing Officer/Director of Nursing.* London: NHS Executive

Summary: the lecturer practitioner role emerged in the 1980s in reponse to the problem of the "theory-practice gap" in nurse education. Less than half the NHS trusts in England have lecturer practitioner posts. Most are employed in the acute sector and most have their contracts with the trusts rather than the associated universities although a large proportion are nevertheless joint-funded. The majority of postholders are female and highly qualified and the reasons for their existence include:

- to promote the connexion between education and service, theory and practice
- to promote research-based practice and develop nursing practice

Recommendations include:

- investigate the cost-effectiveness of the role
- inform reviews of UKCC and government policy
- consider a national framework for teaching practice
- establish means to promote dialogue between health service and higher education
- in order to promote *NHS: a service with ambitions (1996)* develop the role to contribute to multi-professional learning and working, developing partnerships, clinical effectiveness and quality of care
- investigate how trusts without lecturer practitioners address the links between service and education

The National Committee of Inquiry into Higher Education (1997) *Higher education in the learning society.* (chair Ron Dearing) London: HMSO

Summary: the last Conservative government appointed this committee in 1996 to report on long-term developments, including funding arrangements, for higher education in the next twenty years. The proposal that undergraduate students contribute £1,000 towards tuition costs only affected nursing and midwifery students on degree programmes, not diploma students who continued to be funded by bursaries. To encourage prospective candidates to these programmes, the Labour government subsequently stated that degree students would also be eligible for bursaries. The report touches on many other areas of significance to education in the health professions, and recommendations are made that extend to all higher education, some already in place in nursing and midwifery education. Recommendations include:

- encouraging research and increasing the funding to support this
- all university lecturers to have a teaching qualification
- encouraging lifelong learning
- widening access gates so as to encourage those with evidence of appropriate experience even where they have no formal qualifications. This ties in with AP(E)L initiatives and stresses the value of vocational experience and "learning from life"
- encouraging equality of access, including students with disabilities and from minority groups

- widening credit transfer between institutions and disciplines
- encouraging the use of portfolios: this is in line with the ENB and UKCC's PREP requirements
- regular assessment by the Quality Assurance Agency to maintain academic standards

Further reading:
Castledine, G. (1997) Impact of Dearing on the future of nurse education. *British Journal of Nursing* 6(17) 1016
Viccars, A. (1997) Midwifery education: how will the changes in funding affect both the student midwife and the midwifery lecturer? *MIDIRS Midwifery Digest* 7(4) 27-31
Whittle, T. and C. (1997) Get in the right lane. *Nursing Standard* 12(8) 24-5

Council of Deans and Heads of UK Faculties for Nursing, Midwifery and Health Visiting (1998) *Breaking the boundaries: educating nurses, midwives and health visitors for the next millenium: a position paper.* London: Council of Deans and Heads of UK Faculties for Nursing, Midwifery and Health Visiting

Summary: a radical look at the future education of nurses, midwives and health visitors working towards an all-graduate profession that is complemented by a rewarding and clearly structured clinical career. The paper recognises that there are recruitment and retention problems and is concerned about the number of students who complete courses but choose not to register to practice. Skilled individuals should be employed to develop a more regionally driven workforce plan for England.

Other points include:

- regulation, supervision and education of health care assistants are inadequate and should be statutory
- life-long learning should be encouraged
- in the main nurses and midwives are trained to work in hospitals although government policy puts the focus on primary health care
- there are problems of contracting for education where staff are developing clinical academic careers and research
- the Council supports the proposal for a single regulatory body responsible for the protection of the public, self-regulation, standard-setting, and the implementation and regulation of professional conduct
- the Council supports the establishment of an Academy of Faculties to agree standards of advanced practice
- the Council supports a central initiative to evaluate and promote interprofessional education and shared learning

UKCC (1998) *Standards for specialist education and practice.* London: UKCC

Summary: this supersedes the document *The future of professional practice: the Council's standards for education and practice following registration (1994).* The key requirements are:

- the necessity of PREP
- the need for a period under preceptorship
- the requirements for spcialist practice which are: clinical practice and care; programme management and clinical practice development; leadership

The document outlines all the entry standards and learning outcomes for each area of specialist practice.

Royal College of Nursing et al (1998) *Tomorrow's nurses and midwives: charter for nursing and midwifery education.* London: Royal College of Nursing

Summary: an eleven point charter designed to improve conditions for students and their clients. It calls for rights and standards in recruitment and selection; financial support; sickness and maternity leave; learning support; representation; accommodation; learning environment and resources; good teaching; complaints, and appeals procedures; and support with any special requirements of students with impairments.

Warner, Morton et al (1999) *Healthcare futures 2010: report commissioned by the UKCC Education Commission.* Glamorgan: Welsh Institute for Health and Social Care

Summary: a look at the issues of health care in the next 10 years in order to prepare pre-registration nursing and midwifery education for the future.

1. Part A looks at the key elements of future health care such as: demographic changes, the changing nature of the workforce and technology.
2. Part B looks at what are likely to be certain changes as opposed to guesses.
3. Part C describes 3 scenarios of possible future health care: "muddling through" - making the best of things in spite of constraints on expenditure and pressure for efficiency; "economic strength and consumer choice" - high expenditure with greater consumer empowerment and decision-making; "individual choice and the free market" - the NHS reduced to the safety net of a fundamentally private service.
4. Part D offers a series of paradoxes: determinants of the future that may co-exist. These include: emphasis on prevention yet great demand for cure and palliation, demand for high-tech medicine yet demand for complementary therapy, greater incidence of the diseases of old age yet greater demands from younger people. Key issues will definitely include: more older people and diseases of old age, developments in genetics, increase in evidence-based practice, new ways of transferring information, changing roles and expectations in the workforce.

Within education: the common core of competencies should now include an understanding of: epidemiology, genetics, change management and information technology, and nurses and midwives will need to be trained to analyse and synthesise such scientific knowledge as a basis of decision-making.

UKCC (1999) *Fitness for practice: the UKCC commission for nursing and midwifery education.* (chair Leonard Peach) London: UKCC

Summary: the commission was established in 1998 to propose a "way forward for pre-registration education that enabled fitness for practice based on health care need". The principles of Project 2000 remain sound and should continue to underpin pre-registration education but the commission has reservations about recruitment and selection, the gap between theory and practice, practice placements, evaluation of outcomes and joint working between service and education providers

Recommendations:

- increasing flexibility in recruitment so as to attract students of different vocational and academic backgrounds; also increasing the number of graduate places but without turning nursing into an all-graduate profession
- APEL to map academic and practice credits: students who have successfully completed the first year should be able to transfer their academic and practice courses to other credit frameworks
- involving service providers in recruitment and selection
- the common foundation programme to last one year with students able to choose their branch programme either at point of recruitment or during the first year
- closing the theory practice gap by refocusing on outcomes-based competencies, these outcomes to be agreed jointly between service and education providers
- students to keep evidence-based portfolios, and to be assessed on performance in practice
- longer practice placements, reflecting the twentyfour-hour, seven-days a week working practice of the health service
- subject benchmarking in higher education to be run jointly by the QAA and UKCC to address issues specific to nursing and midwifery
- examining the possibility of skills laboratories that would prepare students for practice placements
- service and education providers to formalise support and feedback for mentors and preceptors
- students to be competent to practice at the point of registration and to have three months supervised practice at the end of their programme with full induction and preceptorship on qualification
- service and education providers to agree ownership of the responsibility for practice based education
- education purchasers to appoint an accountable individual to liaise between service and education providers and to support practice placements and contract monitoring
- developing teams of expert practitioners and academic staff to offer advice on clinical practice, management, assessment, mentoring and research

Most proposals can be implemented within two to three years. Issues such as interprofessional learning and teaching, reviewing the branch structure and funding need to be looked at on a longer term basis.

Further reading:
Anon (1999) UKCC education review supports Project 2000. *Nursing Standard* 13(52) 4-5
Munro, R. (1999) Education heads back to basics. *Nursing Times* 95(37) 5
Waters, A. (1999) A little fine tuning. *Nursing Standard* 13(52) 12-13

Department of Health (2000) *A health service of all the talents: developing the NHS workforce.* London: Department of Health

Summary: this review applies to the NHS in England only and is concerned with the roles and responsibilities of NHS staff to maximise quality of patient care, to improve training opportunities and to clarify who should be responsible for workforce planning. Some current weaknesses are identified: not enough attention given to the changing needs of the NHS; not enough flexibility about services, professional roles and training. Four key areas are identified for change:

1. Greater integration, more flexibility: workforce planning should be considered alongside local service needs for primary, secondary and tertiary care. Funding for the education of the different professions should no longer be separate. There should be greater emphasis on skill mix and healthcare worker roles.

2. Better management: local trusts should still develop their own workforce plans; in addition health authorities should contribute to the aims of the Health Improvement Programmes. New Workforce Development Confederations should be established to align the needs of local plans and non-NHS workforce needs, and to liaise with educational institutions.

3. Improved training, education and regulation: there should be flexible, multidisciplinary training routes and programmes for all health professionals. The recommendations of *Making a difference (1999)* to be implemented. Private sector employers should also play a role in training.

4. Staff numbers and career pathways: the workforce has been underestimated and needs to increase and there should be a review of the roles of senior house officers, specialist registrars, consultants and the primary care professions.

These proposals are intended to improve patient care by the inception of true multidisciplinary working and the end of "professional tribes".

Further reading:
Carlisle, D. (2000) Workforce plans see managers in control.
Health Service Journal 110(5700) 7
Glen, Sally (2000) Partnerships: the way forward.
Nurse Education Today 20(5) 339-340

Audit Commission (2001) *Hidden talents: education, training and development for healthcare staff in NHS trusts.* London: Audit Commission

Summary: this covers the education and training of all existing healthcare staff in NHS trusts except dentists and doctors – see *The doctors' tale (1995)*. A partner study conducted by the National Audit Office looks at the provision of education for newly qualified healthcare professionals.

Education and training is commonly provided 'in-house' and by commission through higher education institutions. It covers core and advanced specialist skllls as well as common skills to do with information handling and technology, management, and interpersonal skills. There is a need for consistent education and training because of:
- the national shortage of nurses and other health care professionals in the NHS
- the need to prepare existing staff at all levels to cope with the changes brought about by modernisation
- changes in professional regulation

Twentythree recommendations are aimed at all levels of personnel from individuals to senior management and are designed to promote a commitment to lifelong learning. They are based on the following principles:
- identifying needs
- facilitating education and training
- monitoring, reviewing and evaluating

Further reading:
Munro, R. (2001) Your career development still decided by a postcode lottery. *Nursing Times* 97(9) 10-12

National Audit Office (2001) *Educating and training the future health professional workforce for England.* London: NAO

Summary: where the Audit Commission's report looks at provision for existing NHS staff, this report looks at education and training for new staff – pre-registration. *The NHS plan (2000)* notes that staff shortages are the biggest restraint on the development of the NHS whilst *A health service of all the talents (2000)* shows how underestimates in workforce development and planning have led to these shortages. There are also found to be variations across the country in the cost per student of qualifying and whilst the 20% attrition rates are no worse in health care than any other higher education subject, this represents a waste of resources and the Department of Health therefore set a target of 13% attrition or less. The report offers recommendations to the Department of Health, the NHS, higher education institutions and the Workforce Development Confederations. These come under the headings of:
- better planning and commissioning of education and training
- obtaining value for money
- developing effective inter-agency partnerships

Department of Health (2001) *Working together, learning together: a framework for lifelong learning in the NHS.* London: Department of Health

Summary: taking as its basis the principle that lifelong learning enables staff growth and fulfilment, organisational effectiveness and improvements in patient care, part of the brief of *The NHS plan (2000)* was to modernise education, training and development. Eight chapters cover:

1. core skills
2. the NHS as a learning organisation
3. the provision of opportunities for staff without professional qualifications
4. pre-registration education for all health care professionals: includes joint learning for core skills, flexible entry and exit points, and partnerships between health, education and regulatory bodies
5. post-registration and professional development emphasising consistent standards and work-based learning
6. effective leadership and management
7. everything an organisation needs to promote lifelong learning: mentorship, supervision, investment and electronic delivery: here outlining the role of the proposed NHS University that will offer '24/365' access to learning opportunities
8. a five year plan of action

Further reading:
Department of Health (2001) *'NHS University prospectus'* [WWW] http://www.doh.gov.uk/nhsuniversity/ (11.02.02)

Supplementary Reading

Ballard, Elaine (1997) *Information for caring: a framework for including health informatics in programmes of learning for nurses, midwives and health visitors and other clinical professions.* London: ENB

English National Board (1993) *Guidelines for education audit.* London: ENB

English National Board for Nursing Midwifery and Health Visiting (1994) *Creating lifelong learners: partnerships for care.* London: ENB

English National Board and the Department of Health (2001) *Preparation of mentors and teachers: a new framework for guidance.* London: ENB

English National Board (1996) *Shaping the future.* London: ENB

NHS Service Delivery and Organisation (2002) *'Making a difference: contributions of higher education library and information professionals to the Government's nursing, midwifery and health visiting strategy.' [WWW]* www.uhsl.ac.uk/reports/MADcontents.html (11.02.02)

UKCC (1995) *PREP and you: maintaining your registration: standards for education following registration.* London: UKCC

UKCC (1998) *Guidelines for students of nursing and midwifery.* London: UKCC

UKCC (2000) *Standards for the preparation of teachers of nursing, midwifery and health visiting.* London: UKCC

6 OLDER PEOPLE

Cornwell, Jocelyn (1989) *The consumer's view: elderly people and community health services.* London: King's Fund

Summary: based on clients' views: this report recommends that elderly care should be more responsive. States the need for carers to listen and treat clients as individuals, highlighting the dangers and consequences of patronising elderly people, stereotyping them as a population that burdens the rest of society. This problem is intensified when the client is of an ethnic minority and needs even greater sensitivity owing to loss of status, loss of home and difficulties with communication. The report finds evidence of institutionalised racism and makes practical recommendations about buildings and environment, transport, information about services, getting to know the client, equity, responsiveness and accountability.

Henwood, Melanie (1992) *Through a glass darkly: community care and elderly people.* London: King's Fund

Summary: a critique of community care of the elderly following the white paper *Caring for people (1989)*. Considers:
- demographic changes
- the shift in policy from direct care to home care and support for informal carers
- poor interaction between health and social care provision at all levels
- demand for residential care.

Recommends a clarification of the role of the NHS and responsibilities of the health authorities and development of NHS nursing homes, their providing an excellent model for continuing care.

Neill, June and Williams, Jenny (1992) *Leaving hospital: elderly people and their discharge to community care: report to the Department of Health.* London: HMSO

Summary: small sample research by the National Institute of Social Work Research Unit that set out to describe hospital discharge in terms of organisation of services, assessment of clients, roles of home care workers and to evaluate the effectiveness of discharge services in terms of relevance and impact on the client.

More elderly people are being discharged from hospital quicker and sicker and yet:
- no policies have been written to react to this development
- with scarce resources, conflict has increased amongst managers as well as between health authorities and social services. There is also poor communication between primary and secondary care agencies
- rehabilitation facilities are rare

- although half the local authorities examined had some kind of discharge scheme, even where there was good practice, finance could not be relied on to continue

Recommendations:
- authorities to have written hospital discharge schemes with a single appointed organiser and stable financing
- planning for discharge should begin as soon as possible after admission
- there should be early reassessment soon after discharge
- there should be an established minimum standard of home help to include housework

Walker, Alan (1994) *Half a century of promises: the failure to realise community care for older people.* London: Counsel and Care

Summary: text of the Graham Lecture describing the failure of government policy over fifty years to match "rhetoric with action" on community care and criticising the introduction of market forces. Outlines five deficiencies:

1. "Floodgates mentality": by providing a full service, governments fear that informal carers would cease to care. In fact informal care is relied on so heavily that relations are likely to break down, leaving the state with an even greater demand for help.
2. Limited conception of community care: no analysis of what community care means or comprises. Health and housing excluded from the social services definition and there have been endless failed attempts at coordination. Care of the elderly is always "ghettoised".
3. Service is provider-led instead of user-led, leading to professional dominance of the service. A frail, elderly person is in no position to "shop around" and choose what they want or pull out of what they don't want. The private sector has equivalent power but not a competitive standard or equivalent responsibility. If they go out of business, the public sector must pick up the pieces.
4. Age discrimination: social services departments monopolised by child care; institutional care for the elderly is deemed acceptable although it was rejected for children fifty years ago; concepts that are applied to the care of the young such as normalisation and integration are forgotten when considering the elderly; care of the elderly takes low priority.
5. Market principles can't work because there are not multiple purchasers and providers and besides, quality should count more than merely who provides.

Proposals:
- a genuine investment in home care is more economical than institutional care
- end discrimination
- older people to have the right to self-determination: managers and providers must be trained to empower service users
- introduce general taxation to finance long-term care and end the division between health and social care

Department of Health (1996) *A new partnership for care in old age (cm 3242).* London: HMSO

Summary: in view of the present cost to individuals of long term care (as much as £20,000) this consultation paper proposes a partnership between individual and state to provide for long term care in old age. The Government has to:
- promote awareness of what a person needing care might face by way of means testing and the cost to themselves
- encourage individuals to make their own provision for care
- encourage the finance industry to offer services that will allow for the provision of care

Audit Commission (1997) *The coming of age: improving care services for older people.* London: Audit Commission

Summary: a report following two studies in continuing care and commissioning community care. The first half of the report concerns assessing and arranging care. The recommendations are:
- health authorities and social services to agree on their respective responsibilities
- there should be a coordinated approach to assessment
- discharge delays to be audited and an individual appointed to monitor process
- time standards to be agreed in fulfilling a care arrangement
- clients and their carers to be kept better informed and involved by social services
- home care services to be reviewed regularly by social services
- care managers to be given greater power and financial control

All of these are considered urgent, short-term actions.

The other half of the report concerns "rebalancing" services so that care is delivered appropriately:
- health authorities and social services to "map" what services are available to them and review what services are really needed
- mapping and review processes to be backed up by an information package that will allow for easy updating
- health authorities and trusts to consider ways of reducing hospital admissions and improving rehabilitation
- social services to improve relations with the independent sector
- social services to develop financial mechanisms and consider ways of rewarding good practice
- social services to develop more "watertight" monitoring processes

All of these are considered "medium term" actions. Three further Audit Commission reports in 2000 look at particular aspects of elderly care, see below.

Further reading:
Littlechild, Rosemary, and Glasby, Jon (2001) Emergency hospital admissions: older people's perceptions. *Education and Ageing* 16(1) 77-90

Clinical Standards Advisory Group (1998) *Community health care for elderly people.* (chair June Clark) London: Stationery Office

Summary: a commissioned report involving visits to sample NHS trusts, interviews with providers and users of services as well as carers; and a prospective study of a small sample of patients following their discharge from hospital.

Main findings:
- great variability in range, level and quality of service
- gaps in the provision of service including physiotherapy, rehabilitation, respite care and equipment
- poorly managed hospital discharge
- poor coordination and understanding between health and social services
- inappropriate use of private care in nursing and residential care homes
- problems with process and outcomes of contracting for community health services

Recommendations:
- there should be published minimum standards of provision
- skill mix of community staff to be reviewed and local criteria published for availablility of and eligibility for services
- greater effort to improve discharge procedures, fulfilling existing policies where these are deemed adequate
- based on categories of need, distinctions between health and social care to be clearly defined
- nursing care to be NHS funded in preference to saving money using private services. Private care as a whole subject to greater regulation; the *Registration of Homes Act 1984* to be reviewed
- drawn up in consultation with the professionals who deliver the service, there should be longer-term, "clinically relevant" contracts for community health services

Further reading:
Newton, John (1998) The muddle of community health care for the elderly. *British Journal of Community Health Nursing* 3(2) 60

Clark, Heather Dyer, Sue and Horwood, Jo (1998) *That bit of help: the high value of low level preventative services for older people.* Bristol: The Policy Press and London: Joseph Rowntree Foundation

Summary: the report of a study that assessed the value of low level helping services. These amount to help with gardening, laundry and about the house. The participants in the study see these services as 'help' not 'care' and as vital in letting them remain at home and out of expensive residential care. The continuing relationship with the helper is also important. The report dislikes the distinction between the value put upon 'high level' personal care and 'low level' domestic help and challenges the low priority given to the "unskilled" help since participants —especially older women- showed a consistently high regard for the skills involved. Recommendations include:

- policy makes and service providers to look beyond the short term and reconsider the value of 'low level' help
- monies for these services might be ring-fenced
- a tool is needed to measure cost-effectiveness and prove the worth of preventive strategies

Further reading:
Clark, H. (1998) Keeping the house up. *Community Care* 16.7.1998 22-23

Health Advisory Service 2000 (1999) *Not because they are old: an independent inquiry into the care of older people on acute wards in general hospitals.* London: Department of Health

Summary: results of an inquiry, listing a catalogue of shortcomings in the acute care of the elderly. These include:
- long periods of waiting in discomfort
- neglected ward environments and a lack of basic supplies
- staff shortages and heavy work loads leading to poor communication and failure to respect privacy and dignity
- problems with food, feeding and nutrition
- problems with discharge planning and care

Recommendations include:
- full involvement in planning of care
- combating the negative attitude that associates old age with ill health
- prejudices and marginalisation of older people to be tackled in terms of range and quality of services
- role of ward manager to be promoted and safe staffing levels and skill mix to be assured
- named individual responsible for feeding and nutrition
- access to specialist knowledge assured twentyfour hours a day, seven days a week
- promotion of a *National Service Framework for Older People* to determine standards of care (see below)

Royal Commission on Long Term Care (1999) *With respect to old age: long term care - rights and responsibilities (cm 4192).* (chair Stewart Sutherland) London: The Stationery Office

Summary: current provision for long-term care cares for the poorest whilst impoverishing those with medium assets and driving many into residential care when this may not be the best option. On the principle that paying for care should be fair and shared between state and individual the report recommends:
- costs should be split between personal care and the costs of housing and living. Personal care to be assessed and determined according to need and covered by general taxation. Housing and living costs to be subject to a means-determined co-payment based on a person's income and savings

- a National Care Commission should be established to monitor and advise on trends and developments

The report dismisses long term care pensions schemes as putting an unfair burden on the young and also notes that: the role of housing will become increasingly important; there should be support for informal carers and that the role of advocacy should be developed.

Further reading:
The other agenda (editorial) (1999) *Community Care* 4.3.1999 15
Mangan, Paul (1999) With respect to old age.
British Journal of Community Health Nursing 4(4) 160
Kohler, Mervyn (1999) Organising the long term care of elderly people.
British Journal of Nursing 8(3) 129

Department of Health (2000) *The NHS plan: the Government's response to the Royal Commission on Long Term Care (cm4818-II).* London: The Stationery Office

Summary: the Government broadly accepts the Commission's recommendations outlined in *With respect to old age (1999)*. The chief exceptions are that the Government sees no need to establish the cost of supporting residential care, and whilst nursing care in care homes is to be free, personal care is not.

Further reading:
Anon (2000) Blow to elderly care, say nurses. *Nursing Times* 96(31) 7

Audit Commission (2000) *Fully equipped: the provision of equipment to older or disabled people in England and Wales.* London: Audit Commission

Summary: this report starts with the premise that efficient equipment services promote independence and improve quality of life. It looks at whether the service is providing value for money and whether it is effective in giving independence to users. The report finds that provision varies widely and does not relate well to demand. Problems include poor quality of equipment, small fragmented services without leadership or management and poor cost-effectiveness when service processes do not meet users' initial needs and have to be repeated. Recommendations:

- local health authorities to have a central specialist service for complex problems and should provide support and leadership to local, less specialised services
- National Priorities Guidance should include these services
- standards of good practice should be established by users, professionals and suppliers
- trust managers to establish quality improvement plans for those equipment service providers that have been identified as substandard by user surveys, local audits or management reviews

Further reading:
Audit Commission (2002) *Fully equipped 2002: assisting independence.* London: Audit Commission

Audit Commission (2000) *Forget me not: mental health services for older people.* London: Audit Commission

Summary: this is another of the series of reports promoting the independence of older people. (see *The coming of age – 1997*) The six chapters cover:
- the nature of mental health problems in old age
- how people get access to services and how to support carers and service providers
- the range of services available in the community
- the range of services available in hospital and residential care
- the need for good communication and coordination between the agencies using the Care Programme Approach
- the need for strategic planning

For the first time, auditors have been appointed to audit mental health services for older people in England and Wales.

Further reading:
Benbow, Susan M. and Lennon, Sean P. (2000) Forget me not: mental health services for older people. *Psychiatric Bulletin* 24(11) 403-4

Audit Commission (2000) *The way to go home: rehabilitation and remedial services for older people.* London: Audit Commission

Summary: another in the series of reports promoting independence for older people. Rehabilitation provision is not consistent or reliable in this country, even though it promotes independence and lessens unnecessary admissions to nursing and residential homes. The report defines the nature and scope of rehabilitation and gives examples of good practice in acute, intermediate and community-based service. The recommendations include:
- trusts to set up and/or develop stroke units
- acute, intermediate and community-based services to be coordinated with a care pathway approach
- there should be good multidisciplinary teamworking with effective communication especially at times of transfer
- trusts to develop screening and assessment services
- good workforce planning and development
- close involvement of health and social care services with geriatricians
- financial flexibility to enable new initiatives

Deeming, Chris (2001) *A fair deal for older people? Public views on the funding of long-term care.* London: King's Fund

Summary: the result of a public opinion poll following the *NHS plan: the Government's response to the Royal Commission on Long Term Care (2000)*. There was wide support for the Government's decision to offer free nursing care but most did not agree with means-testing those people who need personal care. Wealthier respondents were in the majority among those willing to pay.

Department of Health (2001) *National service framework for older people.* London: Department of Health

Summary: following *A first class service: quality in the new NHS (1998)* this detailed document sets eight standards for the health and social care of older people. Each standard outlines an aim, a definition and a standard rationale with key interventions and a timescale for completion. The eight standards cover:

1. age discrimination
2. person-centred care
3. intermediate care: bridging the gap between acute and primary services
4. general hospital care
5. stroke
6. falls
7. mental health
8. health promotion

A separate document covers the medicines-related aspects of the NSF. Guidelines are offered for local implementation and national support.

Further reading:
Age Concern England (2001) *Age Concern's response to the NSF for older people.* London: Age Concern England
Black, D. (2001) NSF preview. *Geriatric Medicine* 30(1) 11-4
Davies, C. (2001) Nursing blueprint for elderly care. *Nursing Times* 97(9) 24-6
Department of Health (2001) *Medicines and older people: implementing medicines-related aspects of the NSF for older people.* London: Department of Health
Lothian, Kate and Philip, Ian (2001) Maintaining the dignity and autonomy of older people in the healthcare setting. *British Medical Journal* 322(7287) 668-70
Wellard, Sarah (2001) Framework marks assault on age discrimination. *Community Care* 5.4.2001 10-11

Roberts, E. Robinson J. and Symour, L. (2002) *Old habits die hard: tackling age discrimination in health and social care.* London: King's Fund

Summary: the result of a confidential telephone survey of health and social service managers in England. The report finds that ageism is endemic, difficult to identify and whilst most managers are responding positively to the *National Service Framework for Older People (2001)* the timeframe is tight with resources and support inadequate. Social services are traditionally managed by age group, with older people given fewer choices and a more basic level of care. On the other hand expectations are lower: on the whole older people and their families were reluctant to complain about their care. Recommendations include:

- make clear the meaning and consequences of ageism
- develop benchmarking
- develop education and training for staff

- legislate to outlaw age discrimination in health and social care
- examine national social policies in order to rule out ageism

Further reading:
Scott, H. (2000) Age discrimination should be outlawed in the NHS. *British Journal of Nursing* 9(1) 4
Tonks, A. (1999) Medicine must change to serve an ageing society: eradicate age discrimination and increase resources. *British Medical Journal* 319(7223) 1450-1

Age Concern and ICM (2002) 'Omnibus survey results' [WWW] http://www.ageconcern.org.uk (16.1.02)

Summary: an Age Concern-commissioned survey about attitudes to the elderly in the UK. Findings include:

- 70% thinks that discrimination exists in our society of whom 58% of those over 65 think it exists
- 65% think that age discrimination should be outlawed
- of those between fifty five and sixty four, 31% believed they had been discriminated against at work
- 14% suffered verbal ageist abuse 17% of those between fifty five and sixty four had been so abused
- 11% have felt discriminated against in their health care or with health care insurance because of their age
- 22% feel that the elderly are poorly represented in the media

Further reading:
Formosa, Marvin (2001) Exposing ageism. *BOLD* 11(2) 15-23
Palmore, Erdman (2001) The ageism survey: first findings. *The Gerontologist* 41(3) 572-75

Supplementary Reading

Bowers, Helen et al (1999) *Standards for health and social care standards for older people.* London: Health Advisory Service 2000 and Brighton: Pavilion Publishing

Centre for Policy on Ageing (1996) *A better home life: a code of practice for residential and nursing home care.* (chair Lady Avebury) London: Centre for Policy on Ageing

Department of Health (2001) *Medicines and older people: implementing medicines-related aspects of the NSF for older people.* London: Department of Health

Department of Health (2000) *Out in the open: breaking down the barriers for older people.* London: Department of Health

DHSS Inspectorate (1995) *The abuse of older people in domestic settings.* London: HMSO

Easterbrook, Lorna (1999) *When we are very old: reflections on treatment, care and support of older people.* London: King's Fund

Edwards, Margaret (2000) *Primary care groups and older people: signs of progress.* London: King's Fund

Finch, Jenny and Orrell, Martin (1999) *Standards for mental health services for older people.* London: Health Advisory Service 2000 and Brighton: Pavilion Publishing

Fruin, David for the Social Services Inspectorate (2000) *Getting the right break: inspection of short-term breaks for people with physical disabilities and older people.* London: Department of Health

Hornstein, Zmira et al (2001) *Outlawing age discrimination: foreign lessons, UK choices.* Bristol: The Policy Press for the Joseph Rowntree Foundation

House of Commons Committee of Public Accounts (1995) *National Health Service day hospitals for elderly people in England.* London: HMSO

Qureshi, H. et al (1998) *Overview: outcomes of social care for older people and carers.* London: Social Policy Research Unit

Roberts, Emilie (2000) *Improving services for older people: what are the issues for PCGs?* London: King's Fund

Robinson, Janice (2002) *Age equality in health and social care.* London: Institute for Public Policy Research and the Nuffield Foundation

Royal College of Nursing (1998) *What a difference a nurse makes: an RCN report on the benefits of expert nursing to the clinical outcomes in the continuing care of older people.* London: Royal College of Nursing

Royal College of Nursing (1999) *Restraint revisited: rights, risks and responsibility: guidance for nurses working with older people.* London: RCN

Social Services Inspectorate and Department of Health (1995) *Moving on: report of the national inspection of social services department arrangements for the discharge of older people from hospital to residential or nursing home care.* London: Department of Health

UKCC (1997) *The nursing and health visiting contribution to the continuing care of older people.* London: UKCC

Wade, Barbara (1996) *The changing face of community care for older people: whose choice?* London: Royal College of Nursing

7 CHILDREN

Children Act 1989: chapter 41. London: HMSO

Summary: a comprehensive piece of legislation that seeks to protect the welfare of children by striking a balance between children's rights, parental responsibilities and the duty of the state to protect children who are at risk. The roles of welfare agencies and their relationships with parents are defined. Areas such as: day care, adoption, protection orders, children's homes, fostering and so on are legislated for. The Act came into force in 1991.

Further reading:
Gaskins, Richard (1993) Comprehensive reform in child welfare: the British Children Act 1989 *Social Service Review* 67(1) 1-15
Kent, Paul et al (1990) Guide to the Children Act 1989.
Community Care 19.4.1990 supplement
Rickford, Frances (1992) Happy families. *Social Work Today* 23(38) 20

Hogg, Christine (1989) *The NAWCH quality review: setting standards for children in health care.* London: National Association for the Welfare of Children in Hospital

Summary: a document offering principles and checklists for setting standards on all aspects of child health care including: in-patients, outpatients, accident and emergency departments, diagnostic and support services and preventive child health. Examples of consumer surveys are given. The review notes three principles behind promoting good hospital and health care for children:
- the involvement of parents
- conducive surroundings/ward environment
- good communication between staff and children and their parents

and gives the NAWCH "Charter" as a basis for standard setting. The Charter makes ten statements about the care of children in hospital, most of which have subsequently made their way into the *Patient's charter: services for children and young people (1996).* They include that children should be hospitalised only when necessary; they have the right to have their parents with them as much as possible; they are entitled to information and to be involved in decisions about their treatment; the services should be geared to their needs and they should be treated by specially trained staff.

Further reading:
Galvin, June and Leonard A. Goldstone (1988) *Junior monitor: an index of the quality of nursing care for junior citizens on hospital wards.* Newcastle upon Tyne: Newcastle upon Tyne Polytechnic Products Ltd
Siddle, J. (1991) A voice for children...NAWCH - the National Association for the Welfare of Children in Hospital. *British Journal of Theatre Nursing* 1(6) 4-5

NAWCH (1990) *Setting standards for adolescents in hospital.* London: National Association for the Welfare of Children in Hospital

Summary: the report starts with the recognition that adolescents have needs separate from children and adults, the word implying change in every sense and a growing need for individuality, autonomy and independence. Purchasers and providers are invited to give consideration to: specialised staffing, the need for privacy, links with the outside, a flexible day and so on. The report gives examples of good practice and a "charter for care".

Further reading:
Shelley, H. (1993) Adolescent needs in hospital. *Paediatric Nursing* 5(9) 16-8

Department of Health (1991) *Welfare of children and young people in hospital.* London: HMSO

Summary: this report identifies issues which providers of health services to children need to address in the light of the new structure of purchasers and providers implemented after *Working for patients (1989)*. It contains recommendations for good practice and areas covered include the unique needs of children in hospital, staff and training needs, day and community services, consent to treatment and parental involvement.

Further reading:
Rogers, Rosemary (1991) Action for sick children. *Paediatric Nursing* 3(90) 6-7
Shelley, Pauline (1991) A commitment to children. *Paediatric Nursing* 3(7) 10-11

Thornes, R (1991) *Just for the day: children admitted to hospital for day treatment.* London: Caring for Children in the Health Services.

Summary: this document looks specifically at day case treatment in the overall context of children's health services. It makes recommendations for both purchasers and providers and outlines twelve recommended quality standards in areas such as: admission procedures, environment, nursing support after discharge and parental responsibilities.

Further reading:
Norris, C. (1992) Making the day bearable. *Paediatric Nursing* 4(3) 21-2
Thornes, Rosemary (1992) A spur to action. *Paediatric Nursing* 4(5) 6-7
While, Alison and Janet Crawford (1992) Day surgery: expediency or quality care? *Paediatric Nursing* 4(3) 18-20

Department of Health (1992) *Child protection: guidance for senior nurses, health visitors and midwives.* London: HMSO

Summary: this report outlines where responsibilities lie for child protection by health authorities, senior nurses and other health care staff. It was written in the context of recent legislation such as the *Children Act 1989* and the *NHS and Community Care Act 1990*. It looks at issues surrounding child abuse and protection in general, and in specific settings such as accident and emergency, school nursing, learning disabilities. Contains examples of good practice.

Department of Health and Royal College of Nursing (1992) *The Children Act 1989: what every nurse, health visitor and midwife needs to know.* London: HMSO

Summary: this is a brief summary of the *Children Act 1989* with specific reference to health care. After an outline of the general principles it relates the Act to health authority responsibilities, and those of individual staff with reference to parental rights, children in need, court orders and child protection.

Department of Health (1993) *The rights of the child: a guide to the UN convention.* London: Department of Health

Summary: sets out the rights of children and young people as laid down by the United Nations convention on the rights of the child to which the UK agreed to be bound in 1991. The Government declares its support for the Convention with certain reservations. There is guidance for the public about who to approach if they feel the rights of children are not being met. Units have been set up to monitor adherence to the Convention; their addresses are listed.

Further reading:
Fulton, Yvonne (1996) Children's rights and the role of the nurse. *Paediatric Nursing* 8(10) 29-31
General Assembly of the United Nations (1989) *Convention on the rights of the child.* New York: United Nations
Newell, P. (1993) *The UN convention and children's rights in the UK.* 2nd ed London: National Children's Bureau.

Audit Commission (1993) *Children first: a study of hospital services.* London: HMSO

Summary: although child care in hospital has been discussed and legislated for since 1959, the report states, the service can still fail and its effectiveness is often not questioned. Six principles are identified:
- child and family-centred care
- specially skilled staff
- separate facilities
- effective treatment
- appropriate hospitalisation
- strategic commissioning

Further reading:
Bailey, J. (1996) Children first: the local audit. *Paediatric Nursing* 8(3) 6-7

Thornes, Rosemary (1993) *Bridging the gaps: an exploratory study of the interfaces between primary and specialist care for children within the health service.* London: Caring for Children in the Health Services

Summary: a research study that looks at the quality of care provision as the child moves from one agency to another within the health service. It directs its statements

and recommendations at GPs, commissioners and providers of care, the NHS Management Executive and the Department of Health and these include a need for:
- shared information and knowledge
- equity of service
- the service to be delivered as close as possible to home
- parents to be clear about who is providing what service and what care they themselves must provide

Further reading:
Rogers, Rosemary (1993) A seamless service? *Paediatric Nursing* 5(2) 5

Hogg, Christine (1994) *Setting standards for children undergoing surgery.* London: Action for Sick Children

Summary: the report offers thirteen standards to purchasers and providers of child care in surgery. These include: the need for specially skilled staff, consent to treatment, preparation for the operation, parents visiting the anaesthetic and recovery rooms, post-operative care, and discharge procedures.

Department of Health (1994) *The health of the nation: a handbook on child and adolescent mental health.* London: HMSO

Summary: this booklet states that while severe mental illness is rare in children and adolescents, between 10 and 20% may need help with mental health problems. Untreated problems cause distress to the child and all who care for them and can lead to severe problems in adulthood as well as an increased demand on public services. The guide offers an action plan for providers, a prevalence table of problems (anorexia, enuresis, phobias etc) and a list of contacts.

Further reading:
Whitfield, W. (1995) Stemming the rising tide. *Paediatric Nursing* 7(4) 16-7

The Allitt inquiry: independent inquiry relating to the deaths and injuries on the children's ward at Grantham and Kesteven General Hospital during the period February to April 1991. (1994) (chair C. Clothier)
London: HMSO

Summary: the document details the circumstances leading up to the killing of four children and injury to nine children by nurse Beverley Allitt in the spring of 1991. Each incident is documented together with the responses to the attacks. Beverley Allitt's training into the profession and her subsequent appointment to the children's ward are discussed as well as staffing levels and ward management at the time of the incidents. In the light of the findings, thirteen recommendations are made including several in the area of nurse recruitment.

Further reading:
Lunn, J. (1994) Implications of the Allitt inquiry...pre-employment health screening and its relationship to psychiatric illness. *British Journal of Nursing* 3(5) 201-2
MacDonald, A. (1995) Lest we forget. *Paediatric Nursing* 7(9) 10-11

MacDonald, A. (1996) Responding to the results of the Beverley Allitt inquiry. *Nursing Times* 92(2) 23-5
Rogers, R. (1994) Lessons to be learned...on the inquiry team into the Allitt Tragedy. *Nursing Standard* 8(29) 18-9
Wooster, P. (1994) The Clothier report. *Modern Midwife* 4(11) 32

Royal College of Nursing (1994) *The care of sick children: a review of the guidelines in the wake of the Allitt inquiry.* London: Royal College of Nursing

Summary: this report aims to raise the profile of paediatric services and to increase pressure on purchasers and providers of these services to raise the standards of service. Areas covered include: community and all types of hospital care, services for black and ethnic minorities, staffing, the education of paediatric nurses, and child health service management.

Further reading:
Leenders, F. (1995) Malevolent intervention. *Paediatric Nursing* 7(9) 6-7

Audit Commission (1994) *Seen but not heard: co-ordinating community child health and social services for children in need: detailed evidence and guidelines for managers and practitioners.* London: HMSO

Summary: this report reviews the problems that have arisen between health and social services in the provision of child care as a result of the *NHS and Community Care Act 1990*. A plan of action is proposed to ensure a closer collaboration and includes the introduction of joint child service plans. The report focuses on the areas of child protection, children looked after by social services, immunisation, family support, day care and child health surveillance.

Further reading:
Notter, J. (1994) Audit Commission report leaves many questions unanswered. *British Journal of Nursing* 3(12) 596-7
Professional Briefing 3 (1995) Co-ordinating community child health services. *Health Visitor* 68(3) 112-5

Department of Health (1996) *The patient's charter: services for children and young people.* London: Department of Health

Summary: a booklet outlining the rights, standards and expectations of children in health and sickness and with special needs. They include the right to see a doctor in confidence; the right to explanations and involvement in discussions and decisions about treatment, the right to be accompanied by a parent when in hospital, and to a named nurse, education, effective pain relief, nice food and so on.

Further reading:
Glasper E.A. and Powell, C. (1996) The challenge of the children's charter: rhetoric vs reality. *British Journal of Nursing* 5(1) 26-9
Leenders, F. (1996) An overview of policies guiding health care for children. *Nursing Standard* 10(28) 33-8
Moores, Y. (1996) What's new for children?...the new patient's charter and services for children. *Nursing Standard* 10(26) 20-1

NHS Executive (1996) *Child health in the community: a guide to good practice.* London: Department of Health

Summary: a guide that quotes the British Paediatrics Association's assertion that the purpose of child health services is to enable as many as possible to reach adulthood "uncompromised by illness, environmental hazard or unhealthy lifestyle". Good practice is outlined in all areas of community health including: health visiting, mental health, school nursing, immunisation, child protection and so on. It states that the keys to good practice are parenting, recognition that children and adolescents have distinct needs and targeting where a service is really needed. Purchasers and providers should take as their basis of care: *The Children Act 1988*, the *UN convention on the rights of the child (1989)* and the *Patient's charter (1991)*. A coordinated relationship between secondary and community care is suggested as well as closer collaboration with other agencies such as local education authorities and social services.

Royal College of Paediatrics and Child Health and the Joint British Advisory Committee on Children's Nursing (1996) *Developing roles of nurses in clinical child health.* London: Royal College of Paediatrics and Child Health

Summary: this document supports the extended role of the nurse in clinical child care and offers thirteen recommendations including:

- research into clinical performance in order accurately to allocate funds
- professional recognition for nurses taking on extended responsibilities
- good collaboration with other professionals and secure lines of communication
- defined quality outcome measures
- effective education and training

Managerial professional and financial commitment is essential to secure these developments.

Hogg, Christine (1996) *Health services for children and young people: a guide for commissioners and providers.* London: Action for Sick Children

Summary: this pack of four booklets update the NAWCH: *Setting standards for children in health care (1989)*. They cover: principles for commissioning and providing services; health promotion, illness and disability and examples of audit with checklists. Good practice is promoted in key areas such as hospital services, child health services in the community and child and adolescent mental health. The document emphasises the importance of recognising children's specific needs and of cooperation between health authorities and social services.

Further reading:
Rogers, R. (1996) Health authorities fail to get the message...new guidance on commissioning health services for children and young people. *Paediatric Nursing* 8(1) 3

Hogg, Christine (1997) *Emergency services for children and young people: a guide for commissioners and providers.* London: Action for Sick Children

Summary: although children and young people are major users of emergency services, few hospitals make special arrangements by providing suitably qualified staff or a child friendly environment. The report proposes an unbroken chain of care covering primary care, accident and emergency departments, children's services and child and adolescent mental health services. There should be a trained children's nurse available in the accident and emergency department for all shifts and suitably qualified and experienced medical staff available at all times. A dedicated mental health team should be on call. Practical advice is given for commissioners on principles of emergency services, community emergencies, accident and emergency departments and ambulance services. There are audit checklists and questionnaires designed to obtain feedback from patients and their families.

Further reading:
New guidance on emergency services. (1997) *Paediatric Nursing* 9(6) 4
Scott, G. (1997) Children in need. *Nursing Standard* 11(40) 14

Royal College of Paediatrics and Child Health (1997) *Witholding or withdrawing life saving treatment in children.* (chair Neil McIntosh) London: Royal College of Paediatrics and Child Health

Summary: a report offering guidelines to the medical profession about when to consider the withdrawal of treatment. five circumstances are described:
- when the child is brain dead
- when the child is in a persistent vegetative state
- when treatment would delay death but not relieve suffering
- if survival would leave the child with unreasonable disability
- if child and family feel that further treatment would cause unbearable suffering

The report's basis is that the child's interests come first and that every effort must be made to bring about a consensus between doctors, parents and the child.

House of Commons Health Committee Reports (1997)

These considered the specific health needs of children and adolescents and the extent to which they are being met by the NHS. Common themes were that health services for children are not always designed to meet the specific needs of the child; services both within the NHS and between health, social and education are often fragmented; appropriate, accurate information on healthcare interventions and outcomes essential for planning, providing and evaluating services is often unavailable or inaccessible; advice and guidance on good practice is often not implemented; services are not always provided by appropriately educated and experienced staff. Services for adolescents should be given greater priority and focus. The transfer of young people from child to adult services requires specific attention. The Committee recommended that the Department of Health should study models of child health services to establish a model of coordinated care; and that purchasers' contract specifications must insist that children's services comply with Department of Health good practice guidance.

House of Commons Health Committee (1997) *The specific health needs of children and young people: second report of the Health Committee: session 1996-97: Vol 1: report together with the proceedings of the Committee.* London: The Stationery Office

Summary: emphasises that children's health needs are significantly different from those of adults' but are not given sufficient priority by policy makers and health service professionals. Changes in attitude, not just policy are required. The Committee found that some major recommendations of the Court report had still not been implemented. Areas of concern are the still high deaths and injuries from road traffic accidents and accidents generally. Recommends that the Department of Health improves data collection and research on childhood accidents and their prevention. Respiratory and infectious diseases are still a problem with the increase in asthma particularly a cause for concern. Although mortality has decreased, children often live longer with chronic conditions that require further care. Mental health problems may be increasing. There is a lack of data on variations in child health by region and social class but the Department of Health is commissioning further research into this. The Committee supports Brititsh Paediatric Association and Association of the British Pharmaceutical Industry recommendations to stop administration of unlicensed or off-label medicines to children. Recommends that the Department of Health should work with the Department of Education and Employment to assist development of services for autistic children. Effective methods of early screening for eye abnormalities should be evaluated.

Further reading:
Roe, M. (1997) Health services for children. *Paediatric Nursing* 9(3) 6-7
Williams, K. (1997) Call for qualified child nurses. *Nursing Standard* 11(24) 14

House of Commons Health Committee (1997) *Health services for children and young people in the community: home and school: third report of the Health Committee: session 1996-97: report together with the proceedings of the Committee.* London: The Stationery Office

Summary: discusses the work of community children's nursing services (CCNS); health services for children at school; legal liability in respect of untoward accidents; respite care; provision of equipment; fragmentation of existing services for children; inter-agency cooperation; combined and integrated child health services. The report summarises the types of education and training available to nurses in relation to child health. It found that very few nurses are qualified in the care of children and of those that are, 25% do not work with children. Not enough is done to capitalise on the skills of qualified nurses, which indicates the low priority given to children's health. Commends the CCNS but found provision varies and calls for expansion. Recommends the gradual expansion to an integrated CCNS that would have 'responsibility for the whole range of children's nursing including health promotion, health assessment and hands on care' and would include mental health nursing for children. CCNS education should be commissioned on the same basis as health visitors and district nurses. Points out the limitations of the existing school health service. The needs of children with chronic health disorders requiring clinical interventions need urgent attention. Recommends the government establishes a Cabinet Sub-Committee on Children and Young People "to review, develop and co-ordinate the Government's policy and strategy on issues of special concern to children and young people".

Further reading:
Casey, A. Young, L. Rote, S. (1997) Integrated nursing services for children. *Paediatric Nursing* 9(5) 8
Whiting, M. (1997) Community children's nursing: a bright future? *Paediatric Nursing* 9(4) 6-7

House of Commons Health Committee (1997) *Child and adolescent mental health services: fourth report of the Health Committee: session 1996-97: report together with the proceedings of the Committee.* London: The Stationery Office

Summary: looks at provision of care in child and adolescent mental health services (CAMHS) and recommends improvements to a service which has been neglected as a priority are within the NHS. Examines range and prevalence of relevant conditions found in younger people and discusses external factors affecting mental health. Looks in particular at suicide, conduct disorder, eating disorders and the difficulties in agreeing on definitions of mental health problems. Evidence of some increase in mental health problems.

Provision of CAMHS is unsatisfactory with failures of liaison and coordination between the agencies involved. Current provision is inadequate both in quality and geographical spread. Recommends that service provision be based on four-tier model and that the Department of Health takes active steps to encourage the adoption of this model across the country to reduce problems of commissioning and inter-agency cooperation.
The four-tier model sets out four levels of care:

1. primary care
2. mental health professionals working solo
3. multi-disciplinary teams
4. in-patient units and highly specialised clinics

First tier is seen as vital in identifying and preventing problems at an early stage. NHS Executive should collect information on current provision and distribution of specialist services. Department of Health should remedy poor data gathering and assessment. Cabinet sub-committee on children and young people should include mental health. CAMHS and other children's services should be brought closer together in an integrated and combined children's health service.

Further reading:
Hodges, C. (1997) A model for change. *Mental Health Nursing* 17(3) 28-9
Symington, R. (1997) Mental health services for young people: inadequate and patchy. *Paediatric Nursing* 9(7) 6-7

House of Commons Health Committee (1997) *Hospital services for children and young people: fifth report of the Health Committee: session 1996-97: report together with the proceedings of the committee.* London: The Stationery Office

Summary: looks at the extensive advice and guidance available on standards of care and finds that the implementation of this guidance is patchy. Each purchasing health authority should have a lead commissioner for child health services and the report calls for more effective monitoring of health authority decisions; accident and emergency services should have separate facilities and trained staff for children, but these are not universally available; general surgeons should not operate on small numbers of children and children should not be admitted to adult wards; tertiary services should be organised on a regional level for rarer more complex conditions. The report endorses the principles of *The welfare of children and young people in hospital (1991)* and believes that children should not be in hospital unless absolutely necessary. The needs of children are significantly different from adults and there should be a strong managerial and clinical focus on children's needs across the whole hospital. The child must be the focus and the service must be designed to meet their needs and be needs-led. Recommends improved data collection as the information necessary to plan and provide child-centred cost-effective services is often not available. Many hospitals fail to meet Department of Health standards on trained staff and so the report recommends maintaining an increase in training places for children's nurses for at least five years.

National Co-ordinating Group on Paediatric Intensive Care (1997) *Paediatric intensive care "A framework for the future": National Co-ordinating Group on Paediatric Intensive Care Report to the Chief Executive of the NHS Executive.* London: NHS Executive

Summary: the current service has developed in an ad hoc, unplanned way and is provided in a range of different settings many of which are very small units. Specialist retrieval units are limited. There are insufficient trained paediatric intensive care (PIC) clinicians and nurses. The report therefore recommends:

- audits of current service to establish the need for PIC
- organisation of service delivery in four types of hospital: district general, lead centres, major acute hospitals and specialist hospitals
- compliance with standards such as training, competencies and facilities for families. An action plan recommends immediate cessation of extra single isolated beds: children needing intensive care should not be nursed on general children's wards
- there should be a designated lead centre in each area: children should not be cared for in centres which do not meet the report's standards
- there should be a twentyfour-hour staffed retrieval service in each geographical area
- protocols on service organisation and management should be developed

Chief Nursing Officer (1997) *A bridge to the future: nursing standards, education and workforce planning in paediatric intensive care: report of the Chief Nursing Officer's taskforce.* London: NHS Executive

Summary: stands alongside the report *A framework for the future (1997)* and endorses the organisation of services into four types of hospital proposed in that report. Addresses nursing issues of standards, education and workforce planning in paediatric intensive care (PIC). Gives key nursing standards for properly resourced PIC according to levels of care required. It proposes more flexible training programmes, more post-registration students on ENB 415, training in retrieval, advanced life-support courses and skills maintenance programmes to ensure sufficient PIC nurses will be available to staff the new framework. The nature of PIC with its fluctuating workload dictates a flexible approach to workforce planning, and optimising the contribution of PIC nurses across the whole framework of children's care, by ensuring skills are maintained and updated, and by establishing professional development programmes. Agenda for action recommends endorsement of standards, training requirements and workforce planning policies described in the report.

Utting, William (1997) *People like us: the report of the review of safeguards for children living away from home.* London: The Stationery Office

Summary: this report arose from the revelations of abuse in children's homes over the preceding twenty years. It studies the residents of children's homes, children in foster care, in boarding schools, penal settings and hospitals in an attempt to formulate a protective strategy. It is especially concerned with the welfare of particularly vulnerable groups of children such as children in care, very young children, children with disabilities, children with behavioural and emotional difficulties and children with parents overseas. The report looks at the hazy area of responsibility: when and whether parents, government or local authorities should be legally responsible for children in different specific situations. Another area is how the criminal justice sytem protects children from abuse, claiming that it does not always do so effectively or with sensitivity.

A protective strategy is proposed, including the following points:
- to deter abusers: a higher entry threshold for paid and voluntary workers
- overall excellence and vigilance towards abuse in management
- effective disciplinary and criminal proceedures to deal with offenders
- effective and improved communication between agencies about known offenders and abusers
- a constant striving for excellence

Further reading:
Fletcher, K. (1998) Investment in fostering should be the future.
Professional Social Work January 1998 6
Mahony, C. (1997) Symptoms of a sinking service.
Local Government Chronicle 12.12.1997 14

Utting, W. (1998) Sir William Utting highlights the important difficult legal issues which affect children living away from home. *Childright* 143 Jan/Feb 1998 2-4
Willow, C. (1997) CROA supports people like us. *Childright* 142 Dec 1997 18

Viner, Russell and Keane, Mark (1998) *Youth matters: evidence-based best practice for the care of young people in hospital.* London: Action for Sick Children

Summary: provision for physical health care for adolescents is poor, with nurse/physician-led services rather than patient-led and very few dedicated adolescent units. The report offers detailed, evidence-based guidelines on commissioning and providing care, looking at the hospital and ward as environments, inpatient services, staffing and education.

Further reading:
Glasper, A. and Cooper, M. (1999) Hospitals need specialist inpatient adolescent units. *British Journal of Nursing* 8(9) 549

Middleton, Sue Ashworth, Karl and Braithwaite, Ian (1999) *Small fortunes: spending on children, childhood poverty and parental sacrifice.* London: Joseph Rowntree Foundation

Summary: the results of a survey focusing on the lifestyles and living standards of British children. Findings include:

- on average children cost £3000 p.a. most of which comes from their own parents
- food takes the largest proportion of spending with significant amounts going on education and almost no difference between boys and girls; spending increases only slightly with age and yet family credit and foster care allowance calculations are age-related which means that younger children can be seriously disadvantaged
- spending varies according to economic circumstances but not as much as expected; average spending is much higher than income support allowances
- a new "measure of poverty" is described based on items and activities that the majority of parents see as necessities. Significant numbers of children go without because parents can't afford the cost
- parents themselves are more likely to go without than their children, especially lone parents and those that do not work: they will go without clothing, holidays and sometimes food

Further reading:
Boseley, Sarah (1997) Poor parents who go without to feed their children. *The Guardian* 10.7.1997
Wark, Penny and Norton, Cherry (1997) Family fortunes. *The Sunday Times* 13.7.1997

Department of Health (1999) *Protecting children, supporting parents: a consultation document on the physical punishment of children.*
London: The Stationery Office

Summary: a consultation document that seeks to modernise the law relating to the physical punishment of children so as to protect children from harm while maintaining parents' rights of "reasonable chastisement". It recognises that "mild physical rebuke" – smacking – is sometimes appropriate but considers where the line should be drawn with physical punishment. The report recommends adopting the European Court of Human Rights guidelines and offers the following factors for consideration:

- reasons for punishment, persons involved, how soon administered after the event, the vulnerability of the child
- the law could state the some forms of punishment can *never* be deemed reasonable for instance using implements such as canes or belts or any punishment likely to cause head injury (including eyes and ears)
- the law could be changed so that the defence of reasonable chastisement is only available in response to less serious charges i.e. in common assault and not actual or grievous bodily harm
- another option would be to make reasonable chastisement available only to parents and no one else *in loco parentis*

Further reading:
Roberts, M. (2000) Protecting children, supporting parents: gove rnment consultation on physical punishment. *Childright* 163 Jan/Feb 2000 3-5
Underdown, A. (2000) *Protecting children, supporting parents: a response by The Children's Society.* London: The Children's Society

Department of Health, Home Office, Department for Education and Employment (1999) *Working together to safeguard children.*
London: The Stationery Office

Summary: the main framework for these guidelines comes from the *Children Act 1989* and takes into account the *UN Convention on the rights of the child* (ratified by the UK in 1991) and also the *European Convention of Human Rights*. The guidelines are very detailed and aimed at anyone whose work involves them with children and families i.e. the police, the probation service, education, health and social services etc. They stress that all agencies must work together for the welfare and protection of the child. The guidelines include:

- summaries of lessons learnt from cases of abuse and neglect
- advice about how best to operate the child protection processes such as when concerns about a child are raised, when a child is suffering harm, what to do if a child is away from home, what to do if a tragedy occurs, the principles to be followed when working with children and families
- advice about the roles and responsibilities of all those involved, the importance of effective communication and the need for multi-agency training

Further reading:
Department of Health (2001) *Safeguarding children in whom illness is induced or fabricated by carers with parenting responsibilities: supplementary guidance to Working together to safeguard children.* London: Department of Health
Martin, G. (1998) Working together – a consultation paper too far? *Family Law* September 532-41
Morrison, T. (2000) Working together to safeguard children: challenges and changes for inter-agency coordination. *Journal of Interprofessional Care* 14(4) 363-73

Protection of Children Act 1999: chapter 14. London: The Stationery Office

Summary: this Act requires the Secretary of State for Health to keep a *Protection of Children Act List* of individuals considered unsuitable to work with children or persons with mental impairment. This used to be a non-statutory "Consultancy Index List"; the Act makes it statutory but also creates a right of appeal to a new tribunal against inclusion on the list. The Department of Education and Empoyment has run a similar statutory *List 99* and the two lists will be checked together in a 'one stop' system. The Act amends part V of *The Police Act 1977* to allow the Criminal Records Bureau to disclose the criminal records of anyone included on either list. This will make it easier to check on applicants for child care positions.

Further reading:
Corbitt, Terry (2001) On the record. *Primary Care Management* 11(4) 26

Department of Health (1999) *Me, survive, out there? New arrangements for young people living in and leaving care.* London: The Stationery Office

Summary: outlines proposals to help to prepare young people for independent living also clarifying the financial support situation so that young people do not have to leave care until they are ready and willing to do so. The paper proposes arrangements for sixteen-seventeen year olds and eighteen-twentyone year olds and was distributed to an extensive range of agencies to emphasise the fact that a multi-agency approach is needed.

The aim is to try and prepare young people to leave by the age of eighteen or earlier if appropriate whilst ensuring they still have support to fall back on. This entails:
- young people being cared for until they feel ready to cope with life on their own. This means that more children will remain in care until they are eighteen
- more involvement from the education, training and employment sectors
- improved local authority contact with young people formerly in care
- making sure that care leavers move to suitable accommodation thus avoiding homelessness and rough sleeping

Further reading:
Anon (1999) The right support at the right time. *Professional Social Work* Sep 1999 4
Folkard, K (1999) A question of survival. *Roof* Sep/Oct 1999 18
Piper, Mari (2000) *A care leaver's perspective.* London: Department of Health

Children (Leaving Care) Act 2000: chapter 35. London: The Stationery Office

Summary: this Act aims to implement the proposals of *Me, survive, out there? (1999).* It amends the *Children Act 1989,* providing for young people in care to move into independent living. A duty is placed on local authorities not only to assess and meet the needs of eligible young people, but also to assist those formerly in their care in respect of education, employment and training. The local authority has a duty to stay in contact with all these eligible care leavers, including eighteen to twentyone year olds. The Act also simplifies the financial support arrangements for young people. It enables local authorities to accommodate, support and advise those leaving care, and will avoid the situation that has formerly existed whereby care leavers were simply given money and left to fend for themselves.

Further reading:
Bateman, N. (2000) Welfare rights: October benefits revolution? *Community Care* 14.12.2000 29
Rickford, Frances (2000) Help is at hand. *Community Care* 5.7.2000 18-19

Madge, Nicola et al (2000) *Nine to thirteen: the forgotten years?* London: National Children's Bureau

Summary: this takes the view that whilst most children pass through the years from nine to thirteen without incident, this is a period of change from childhood to adolescence when problems may arise for the first time such as delinquency, substance abuse and sexual violence on the one hand, abuse and neglect on the other. The report argues for an increased focus on services for this age group since at this age, it is still possible to stop problems in their tracks.

Department of Health (2000) *Adopting changes: survey and inspection of local councils' adoption services.* London: The Stationery Office

Summary: the results of a national survey conducted by the Social Services Inspectorate, evaluating local councils' adoption services and designed to give a detailed picture of current practice in order to plan for change. The issues are:

- many councils have good adoption practice but in some councils there are children in need of adoptive families who are not found them
- the time taken to identify an adoption varies greatly, the whole process taking anything from six months to four and a half years. Some of these delays arise because of a lack of trained staff and some because of difficulties placing children who have medical problems, disabilities or emotional/behavioural difficulties. However, councils' policies, procedures and practice guidance are by no means universal or consistent; the report states the need to address ALL avoidable causes of delay
- the report also finds that potential adopters were put off by the delay in response in some cases and by the tone of response in others. For many, the whole process took far longer than they were led to expect
- "post-adoption" services are underdeveloped in all areas

Department of Health (2000) *Adoption: a new approach.* London: The Stationery Office

Summary: a white paper that proposes speeding up the adoption process and putting the needs of children first by introducing new legislation and procedures. Amongst these proposals are an investment of £66.5 million over three years and a 40% increase in number of adoptions by 2004/5. Councils are to improve their adoption practices and ultimately achieve a 50% increase in numbers of children adopted. The supporting legislation provides for:

- an adoption register holding details of approved adoptive families and of children waiting for adoption
- a new legal framework for adoption allowances
- an independent review mechanism for assessing potential adopters
- for adoptees: access to information about their history
- the payment of court fees by councils once 'looked-after' children are adopted
- bringing the *Children Act 1989* and the *Adoption Act 1976* into line

There will also be a consultation for National Adoption Standards: aimed at all those involved in the adoption process this will clarify expectations, placing the needs of the child first.

Other proposals include: paid adoption leave for one parent of an adopted child; practice guidelines for councils; a range of powers to deal with councils that fail to provide a reasonable level of service; increased flexibility for courts in the family justice system in specialised adoption court centres.

Further reading:
Anon (2001) Adoption: a new approach. *Childright* no. 173 Jan/Feb 8-10
Rickford, F (2001) Good on paper. *Community Care* 1.2.2001 18-19

Adams, K. (2001) *Developing quality to protect children: SSI inspection of children's services, August 1999 – July 2000.* London: The Stationery Office

Summary: a report summarising the findings of thirty one local inspections of children's services following the Quality Protects initiative. It provides a starting point from which future improvements can be measured.

The quality of the services varied greatly from council to council although no single council was better or worse than the rest as they all had good and bad points. There was evidence that bodies such as education authorities and other health agencies were becoming increasingly involved in the planning and implementation of children's services and the importance of this was widely recognised. The Quality Protects programme was clearly being implemented, only some councils were further 'down the line' than others.

Specific problems were highlighted: in 6% of cases, children requiring protection were considered not to have been adequately safeguarded; this was brought to the attention of senior managers. Another problem was that training was judged to be low or insufficient in areas such as child protection, inter-agency work, assessment work and communicating with children. In many areas however the situation was seen to be improving.

Department of Health *The children's national service framework.*
This project is in progress, due for publication in 2003. Key issues will include:
- Learning from Bristol
- problems with access and inequalities
- children with disabilities and special needs
- involving parents and children in planning care

Updates and more details can be found at www.doh.gov.uk/nsf/children.htm

Supplementary reading:

Audit Commission (2000) *Children in mind: child and adolescent mental health services.* London: Audit Commission

British Paediatric Association (1993) *The care of critically ill children: report of the multidisciplinary working party on paediatric intensive care.* London: BPA

British Paediatric Association (1995) *Health needs of school age children.* (chair Leon Polnay) London: British Paediatric Association

Department of Education and Department of Health (1994) *The education of sick children.* London: HMSO

Department of Health (1994) *Services for mental health of children and young people in England: a national review.* London: HMSO

Department of Health (2001) *The Children Act report 2000.* London: The Stationery Office

Department of Social Services (1988) *Report of the inquiry into child abuse in Cleveland 1987.* (chair Elizabeth Butler-Sloss) London: HMSO

Hall, David M. B. (ed)(1996) *Health for all children: report of the third joint working party on child health surveillance. 3rd ed.* Oxford: Oxford University Press

Hogg, Christine (1998) *Child friendly primary health care.* London: Action for Sick Children

McHaffie, H. E. et al (1999) Witholding / withdrawing treatment from neonates: legislation and official guidelines across Europe. *Journal of Medical Ethics* 25(6) 440-446

NHS Advisory Service (1995) *Child and adolescent mental health services: together we stand: the commissioning role and management of child and adolescent mental health services.* London: HMSO

NHS Management Executive (1994) *Paediatric intensive care.* London: Department of Health

Performance and Innovation Unit (2000) *Prime Minister's review: adoption: issued for consultation.* London: Cabinet Office: PIU

Slater, Mary (1993) *Health for all our children: achieving appropriate healthcare for black and ethnic minority children.* London: Action for Sick Children

Walker, Alison (1996) *Young carers and their families: a survey carried out by the Social Survey Division of the ONS on behalf of the Department of Health.* London: The Stationery Office

8 Midwifery

House of Commons Health Committee (1992) *Second report: maternity services, volume 1.* (chair Nicholas Winterton) London: HMSO

Summary: the main outcome of this report is the shift towards "woman-centred" care and the establishment of the Expert Maternity Group responsible for the subsequent report *Changing childbirth (1993)*. The first chapters trace the history of maternity services this century and consider evidence from organisations (such as the National Childbirth Trust), health professionals and mothers. Previously, women were urged to give birth in hospital maternity units in the mistaken belief that this was safer. The report refutes this belief, advising against the assumption that this is what women want and advocating instead the "three Cs":

- CONTINUITY: of place of antenatal care and birth with known individual midwife
- CHOICE: sufficient information given to enable woman to determine where to give birth and what care she wants (feeding methods, epidurals, caesareans etc)
- CONTROL: women to be able to talk with health professionals and contribute to the decisions about their care during all stages of pregnancy and birth

The report stresses that women's rights take precedence over those of health professionals who must do more to implement the three Cs.

Community-based care to be encouraged: antenatal visits to be made in the home and the systematic closure of rural maternity units to stop.

Maternity care is set in the broad socio-economic context taking into account factors such as diet and maternity leave and considering financial implications such as of providing benefits and income support during pregnancy.

The implications for training are considered (of GPs, obstetricians and midwives), as well as research (National Perinatal Epidemiology Unit) and statistics (of neonatal morbidity and birthweight).

The report recommends that the expertise and status of midwives be recognised, team midwifery be established and midwives given the right to admit women to hospital.

Further reading:
Garrod, D. (1994) Cutting the cord. *Modern Midwife* 4(2) 31-3
Meldrum, P. (1994) Moving towards a common understanding in maternity services. *Midwifery* 10(4) 165-70
Rothwell, R. (1996) Changing childbirth. *Midwives* 109(1306) 291-4
Walton, I. (1994) Adapt and evolve. *Nursing Times* 90(32) 56-7

Department of Health (1993) *Changing childbirth: Part 1: report of the expert maternity group.* (chair Julia Cumberlege) *Part II: Survey of good communications practice in maternity services.* London: HMSO

Summary: an Expert Maternity Group was set up in response to the House of Commons Health Select Committee report *Maternity services (1992)* to review policy on NHS maternity care, particularly during childbirth, and to make recommendations. The objective of the group was to improve NHS maternity services. Report identifies three key principles which must underlie effective woman-centred maternity services and gives the objectives and action points to be met by the purchasers and providers of maternity services. The key principles are:

- the woman is the focus of maternity care. She should be able to feel that she is in control of what is happening to her and able to make decisions about her care, based on her needs, having discussed them fully with the professionals involved
- maternity services must be readily and easily accessible to all. They should be sensitive to the needs of the local population and based primarily in the community
- women should be involved in the monitoring and planning of maternity services to ensure that they are responsive to the needs of a changing society. In addition care should be effective and resources used efficiently

The theme of the report is: "woman-centred care, control, choice and continuity" with an emphasis on the role the midwife is to play in maternity care.

Further reading:
Browne, A. (1994) Are midwives ready for the proposals for change? *Nursing Times* 90(47) 36-7
Everitt, N. (1995) Implementing good practice: the Changing Childbirth implementation team. *British Journal of Midwifery* 3(3) 139-41
Jackson, K. (1995) Changing childbirth: encouraging debate. *British Journal of Midwifery* 3(3) 137-8
Savage, W. (1994) The Mabel Liddiard Memorial Lecture, 1994. Changing childbirth: would Mabel Liddiard approve? *Midwives Chronicle* 107(1282) 411-3

Department of Health (1994) *The patient's charter: maternity services.* London: HMSO

Summary: outlines patients' rights in relation to maternity services, concentrating specifically on: midwifery, obstetrics and paediatrics services; maternity records; antenatal appointments; security in maternity units; pregnancy care.

The document also gives a very brief outline of some of the improvements in maternity services implemented since the publication of *Changing childbirth (1993)*.

English National Board for Nursing, Midwifery and Health Visiting (1995) *Developments in midwifery education and practice: a progress report.* London: ENB

Summary: this report gives a summary of the work of the ENB in helping to implement the targets in *Changing childbirth (1993)* through its educational programmes and monitoring of midwifery practice. ENB representatives carried out practice visits to assess services with particular attention to woman-centred care advocated in *Changing childbirth (1993)*. Around thirty examples of good practice are summarised, under nine headings:

Community oriented care; woman-centred care; midwifery service and management; supervision; professional development; midwifery practice and care; antenatal care; intrapartum care; postnatal care.

The second half of the document gives statistics on how far the different health regions in England have achieved the ten indicators of *Changing childbirth (1993)*.

English National Board for Nursing, Midwifery and Health Visiting (1995) *Midwifery educational resource pack: the challenge of Changing childbirth.* London: ENB.

Summary: this six-volume pack gives endorsement by the ENB for the implementation of *Changing childbirth (1993)*. It stresses the importance of midwifery education in the process, and aims to help midwives develop the skills that will enable them to put the report's recommendations into action. The pack is a useful educational and professional development tool containing reprints of important journal literature and interactive sections such as self-reflection questions and planning exercises. It concludes that *Changing childbirth (1993)* is a great opportunity for the midwifery profession and that in empowering women with choice, midwives empower themselves as health professionals.

Further reading:
Pope, R. (1997) Aspects of care provided by midwives, part 1: an overview. *British Journal of Midwifery* 5(12) 766-70
Pope, R. et al (1998) Aspects of midwifery care, part 2: enhanced role and social aspects. *British Journal of Midwifery* 6(1) 20-4
Pope, R. et al (1998) Aspects of midwifery care, part 3: the organization of midwifery care. *British Journal of Midwifery* 6(2) 88-92
Pope, R. et al (1998) Aspects of care, part 4: views of professionals and mothers. *British Journal of Midwifery* 6(3) 144-7
Pope, R. et al (1998) Aspects of care, part 5: the continuing educational needs of midwives. *British Journal of Midwifery* 6(4) 266-70
Pope, R. et al (1998) Aspects of care, part 6: continuing educational needs of midwives, part 2. *British Journal of Midwifery* 6(5) 298-302

English National Board for Nursing, Midwifery and Health Visiting (1997) *Preparation of supervisors of midwives.* London: ENB

Summary: this four module learning pack came out of the ENB's requirement that midwife supervisors complete a programme of study to ensure quality standards in supervision as well as the care of mothers and babies. It takes into account the proactive and high profile role of supervisors, the recommendations laid out in *Changing childbirth (1993)* and the amended *Midwives rules (1993)*. The four modules cover the following areas:

- supervisors' role
- statutory role
- supporting good practice and professional development
- managing professional conduct

Each module contains interactive activities to be followed in conjunction with supervisors' work.

Further reading:
UKCC (1998) *Midwives rules and code of practice.* London: UKCC

Audit Commission (1997) *First class delivery: improving maternity services in England and Wales.* London: Audit Commission

Summary: this report is the result of surveys carried out amongst maternity care professionals and recent mothers and is aimed mostly at purchasers of maternity care. It looks at how 'woman-centred care' services recommended in *Changing Childbirth (1993)* have been implemented and takes into consideration the impact of clinical effectiveness information and regional differences in services. There are chapters on antenatal, perinatal and postnatal services from the woman's perspective and also from the point of view of service providers. Each chapter ends with recommendations for improvement for trusts, commissioners of services and the NHS Executive.

The central themes are:
- effectiveness information for clinicians and midwives
- improved choice and information for women
- continuity of care and increased role for midwives
- following best practice

Further reading:
Fitzsimmons B (1997) First class delivery: a review of the Audit Commission report. *British Journal of Midwifery* 5(7) 388-92
Robinson J (1997) First class delivery: auditing the auditors. *British Journal of Midwifery* 5(4) 227

English National Board for Nursing, Midwifery and Health Visiting (1998) *Creating lifelong learners: partnerships for care: guidelines for pre-registration midwifery programmes of education.* London: ENB

Summary: this replaces and updates the 1994 document of the same name. It considers the increased role of midwifery supervision, the shift to woman-centred care and the integration of midwifery education into higher education. It states that midwifery programmes must include: the midwifery profession, the midwife and society and midwifery practice.

Further reading:
English National Board and Royal College of Midwives (1997) *A joint statement on midwifery education for practice.* London: ENB
Fraser, D. et al (1997) *An outcome evaluation of the effectiveness of pre-registration midwifery programmes of education.* London: ENB

Department of Health (1998) *Midwifery: delivering our future: report by the Standing Nursing and Midwifery Advisory Committee* (chair Alison Norman). London: Department of Health.

Summary: the theme of the report is the evolving role of the midwifery profession. Changes in maternity services during the 1990s are outlined and their impact on education, supervision, autonomy and professional role of midwives. Influencing factors include woman-centred care, primary care-led NHS, midwives' role in management and cooperation with obstetricians and GPs.

Recommendations include:
- midwifery education should be at graduate level while maintaining shortened courses for registered nurses
- representation of midwives on education purchasing consortia
- access for midwives to clinical effectiveness information
- midwife involvement in management of trusts and commissioners to encourage woman-centred care
- NHS research and development organisations to encourage research in midwifery
- opportunities for professional development and lifelong learning to be available to all midwives
- consideration should be given to prescribing by midwives

Further reading:
Henderson, C. (1998) Midwifery: delivering our future. *British Journal of Midwifery* 6(5) 292-3

Royal College of Midwives (2000) *Vision 2000.* London: Royal College of Midwives

Summary: the "vision" concerns the development of UK maternity services in the light of the new health policies. Whilst models of care vary across the country, the RCM proposes twelve key principles to inform future development. These include:
- woman and family-centred care
- public health: reducing morbidity and promoting equality of access
- community focused care "seamlessly" integrated with acute services
- pregnancy and birth to be viewed as a normal state of health, avoiding unnecessary medicalisation
- midwifery-led care: whilst working in partnership with other professionals and care agencies, strong midwifery leadership will ensure high quality and continuity of care

Further reading:
Gould, D. (2000) Stronger leadership is needed before we can 'own' change. *British Journal of Midwifery* 8(8) 480-81

Supplementary Reading

Abortion Act 1967: chapter 87. London: HMSO

Campbell, R. (1994) *Where to be born? The debate and the evidence. 2nd ed.* Oxford: National Perinatal Epidemiology Unit

Chamberlain, G. (ed) (1994) *The future of maternity services.* London: Royal College of Obstetricians and Gynaecologists.

Congenital Disabilities (Civil Liability) Act 1976: chapter 28. London: HMSO

Department of Health *Confidential enquiry into stillbirths and deaths in infancy (annual).* London: The Stationery Office

Department of Health. *Report on confidential enquiries into maternal deaths in the UK (triennial).* London: The Stationery Office (see also Why mothers die.)

Department of Health (1997) *Learning together: professional education for maternity care.* London: The Stationery Office

Department of Health (1998) *Why mothers die: report on confidential enquiries into maternal deaths in the UK 1994-1996.* London The Stationery Office

English National Board (1997) *Report of midwifery practice audit 1996-97.* London: ENB

English National Board (2001) *Midwifery practice in England: the report of the audit of maternity services and practice visits.* London: ENB

Garcia, J. (1993) *Getting consumers' views of maternity care: examples of how the OPCS survey manual can help.* London: HMSO

Human Fertilisation and Embryology Act 1990: chapter 37. London: HMSO

Maternity Care Working Party (2001) *Modernising maternity care: a commissioning toolkit for primary care trusts in England.* London: RCOG

Midwifery Research database - *MIRIAD: a sourcebook of information about research in midwifery (annual).* Hale, Cheshire: Books for Midwives Press (nb publication ceased from 1998)

Pope, R. (1996) *Identification of the changing educational needs of midwives in developing new dimensions of care in a variety of settings and the development of an educational package to meet their needs.* London: ENB

Redshaw, M. (1996) *Delivering neonatal care: the neonatal unit as a working environment: a survey of neonatal unit nursing.* London: HMSO

Royal College of Obsterics and Gynaecology and Royal College of Midwives (1999) *Towards safer childbirth: minimum standards for the organisation of labour wards : report of a joint working party.* London: RCOG

Royal College of Obsterics and Gynaecology (2001) *Why mothers die: report on confidential enquiries into maternal deaths in the UK 1997-2000.* London: RCOG

Still-Birth (Definition) Act 1992: chapter 29. London: HMSO

9 Mental Health

Department of Health (1983) *Mental Health Act 1983: chapter 20.*
London: HMSO

Summary: amends some of the provisions of the 1959 Act. Coverage includes: access to Mental Health Tribunals; participation of the whole multidisciplinary team (nurses, psychiatrists, psychologists, social workers) in decisions on treatment and detention; consent to treatment; mentally disordered offenders; community and informal psychiatric care.

Further reading:
Dimond, Bridget (1984) The Mental Health Act 1983. *Community Care* 23.2.1984 23-6
Killen, S. (1983) Nurses and the Mental Health Act. *Nursing Times* 79(37) 44-48
Mawson, D. (1986) Seeking informed consent...1983 Mental Health Act.
Nursing Times 82(6) 52-53
Webster, L. Dean, C. and Kessel, N. (1987) Effect of the 1983 Mental Health Act on the management of psychiatric patients. *British Medical Journal* 295(6612) 1529-32

Department of Health Mental Health Nursing Review Team (1994)
Working in partnership:a collaborative approach to care.
(chair A. Butterworth) London: HMSO

Summary: identifies the role of nurses in the mental health team. In particular examines: key workers' role, schizophrenia, elderly mentally ill, advanced nursing practice, research, recruitment and education for mental health nurses and access to information.

Further reading:
Morris, M. (1994) Working in partnership report signals a pivotal role for mental health nurses. *British Journal of Nursing* 3(6) 253-4
Sandford, T.(1994) Working in partnership... Mental Health Nursing Review.
Nursing Standard 8(25) 20-21
Smith, L. N. (1994) A review of the report on mental health nursing in England: working in partnership.
Journal of Psychiatric and Mental Health Nursing 1(3) 179-83

Department of Health (1994) *The health of the nation key area handbook: mental illness. 2nd ed.* London: HMSO.

Summary: expands on the targets in *The health of the nation (1992)* white paper. Recommends improving the health of the mentally ill and reducing suicide rates. Looks at changes in services, treatment methods and settings.

Further reading:
Murdock, D. (1995) Redefining the targets for mental illness.
Nursing Standard 10(49) 28-30

House of Commons Health Committee (1994) *Better off in the community?: the care of people who are seriously mentally ill: 1st report.* London: HMSO

Summary: this report looks at the transition from institutionalised to community care and the closure of institutions. Particular areas covered are: the care programme approach (CPA); safety and security of the public in relation to care in the community of mentally ill patients; the homeless mentally ill; responsibilities of institutionalised care settings; future service patterns to be in place by the year 2000; interdepartmental cooperation between health and social services and closer monitoring of existing community care systems for the mentally ill.

Audit Commission (1994) *Finding a place: a review of mental health services for adults.* London: HMSO

Summary: this report concentrates on services provided for adults with mental health problems. It describes how historically policy has shifted from care in large psychiatric hospitals to care in the community. Concerns over the slow implementation of community care policy are discussed along with the allocation of resources, and the patchy implementation of the care programme approach. The report concludes that the way forward involves strengthening leadership and management, and identifies the main challenges as:
- the correct targeting and management of the service
- reviewing the pattern of resource distribution

The consequences for the commissioning authorities and different agencies is then examined

Further reading
Shepherd, G. (1995) Finding a place: a review of mental health services for adults. *Journal of Mental Health* 4(1) 9-16

Department of Health (1995) *Mental Health (Patients in the Community) Act 1995: chapter 52.* London: HMSO

Summary: this Act is concerned with the care and supervision of patients with mental disorders after their discharge from hospital. It states the criteria under which health authorities may apply for a supervision order, e.g. where a patient may still be considered to be a risk to the safety of himself or others. It updates the 1983 Act on areas such as the role of medical practitioners, and patients' leave of absence from hospital.

Further reading:
Coffey, M. (1996) Supervised discharge...Mental Health Act 1995. *Nursing Times* 92(26) 50-3

Department of Health (1996) *The spectrum of care: local services for people with mental health problems.* London: Department of Health

Summary: handbook summarising the components which constitute the complete range of care that should be available to people with mental illness. Local purchasers of mental health services should ensure that their plans are coordinated with other service providers, that there are clear lines of responsibility and that there is a flexibility of approach to ensure all needs are met. Local mental health services should ensure that the most appropriate treatments are offered from the wide range of medications and psychological treatments. Mental health service providers should offer the most appropriate setting for treatment whether it is based at home, in day care or in a residential setting.

Department of Health (1996) *Building bridges: a guide to inter-agency working for the care and protection of severely mentally ill people.* London: HMSO

Summary: this report aims to encourage inter-agency working. Aimed at mental health professionals, managers and purchasers it provides information about the care programme approach, the current legislative framework and discusses issues such as client confidentiality and information sharing. The report also outlines the roles of the various agencies involved and how they should best work together. There is information about auditing services as well as continuing education and training.

Sheppard, David (1996) *Learning the lessons: mental health inquiry reports published in England and Wales between 1969 and 1996 and their recommendations for improving practice. 2nd ed* London: Zito Trust

Summary: collation of inquiry reports about homicides involving mental health patients. This second edition documents fifty four independent inquiries and over three hundred recommendations. The first half of the publication lists each inquiry with details of the incident and the terms of reference of the inquiry. The second half contains a list of the various recommendations arranged chronologically by subject.

Thornicroft, G. and Strathdee, G. (1996) *Commissioning mental health services.* London: HMSO

Summary: for those involved in purchasing and commissioning mental health services, this report gives information about good practice, current areas of debate and details of population-based service planning. Four sections cover:
- the national policy framework within which commissioning takes place
- the perspectives of purchasers and commissioners
- the commissioning process from the provider's perspective
- the implementation of policy

Department of Health (1997) *The patient's charter: mental health services.* London: HMSO

Summary: a booklet that summarises the principles of the *Patient's charter (1991)* then outlines patients' rights in the context of mental health. Areas covered include confidentiality, the care programme approach, discharge from hospital and an explanation of the *Mental Health Act 1983.* A list of addresses covers organisations concerned with mental health care.

Sainsbury Centre for Mental Health (1997) *Pulling together: the future roles and training of mental health staff.* London: Sainsbury Centre for Mental Health

Summary: report reviews the roles and training of mental health staff working in the community and identifies the knowledge, skills and attributes they need. Major improvements in staff training can be achieved within the framework of existing professions, however there is a need to establish core competencies for all mental health staff and distinctive competencies for each profession. The review lists eight key findings leading to some twenty recommendations, these include:

- a mismatch between current training and service needs
- specialisms should be upheld and extended
- providers should be supported to develop strategies that will ensure continued fitness for purpose
- each professional group should develop occupational standards that are linked to core competencies

Department of Health (1997) *Developing partnerships in mental health (cm3555).* London: The Stationery Office

Summary: a green paper that describes the government's commitment to developing partnerships in the care of people with severe mental illness. The document emphasises the importance of integrating the work of statutory, voluntary and independent agencies to provide a seamless mental health service.

It concludes with options for structural changes and seeks views from interested parties on which approaches would be the most effective. These options are:

- establishing a new mental health and social care authority
- establishing either the health authority or local authority as a single agency
- combining the health and local authorities to create a joint health and social care body
- allowing health and local authorities to delegate functions and responsibilities to each other

Further reading
Ashman, M. (1997) Green, green grass of change. *Mental Health Nursing* 17(2) 4-5

Mental Health Act Commission and Sainsbury Centre (1997) *The national visit: a one-day visit to 309 acute psychiatric wards by the Mental Health Act Commission in collaboration with the Sainsbury Centre for Mental Health.* London: Sainsbury Centre for Mental Health

Summary: a snapshot view of acute inpatient facilities that looked in particular at detained patients who were absent without leave, the care of women patients, and nursing staff. Findings include:

- with the emphasis on care in the community, inpatient care has been neglected
- inpatient care involves a heavy workload and staff were having difficulty ensuring leave was properly authorised

- many women have to share facilities with men, 3% even sleeping in the same area; half the wards reported problems of sexual harassment
- although staffing is adequate, nurses were not always in contact with patients and lacked the skills and support needed to communicate effectively with patients who had severe illnesses such as schizophrenia and manic-depression

The report recommends viewing inpatient and community psychiatric care as an integrated whole, improving management and leadership; updating nurses skills through training and addressing the issue of safety for women patients.

Firth, Malcolm and Kerfoot, Michael (1997) *Voices in partnership: involving users and carers in commissioning and delivering mental health services.* London: The Stationery Office

Summary: this report outlines the challenges to user and carer participation in the development of NHS services for mental health and makes recommendations as to how they are addressed. The report is based on research carried out in 1994-96 on adults using mental health services and their adult carers. The effects of recent legislation, the role of users and carers in service planning and delivery and sources of conflict are considered. Recommendations are made for the way forward. These include employment of salaried workers, training as care/service professionals, mainstream funding and the wider development of professional advocacy for users and carers.

United Kingdom Central Council for Nursing, Midwifery and Health Visiting (1998) *Guidelines for mental health and learning disabilities nursing.* London: UKCC (see Chapter 10 Learning Disabilities)

Department of Health (1998) *Tackling drugs to build a better Britain: the government's ten year strategy for tackling drug misuse.*
London: The Stationery Office

Summary: building on the previous government's strategy *Tackling drugs together (1995)*, this report aims to take a new long-term approach to the drugs issue. The new strategy is based on an extensive review by the recently appointed UK anti-drugs coordinator, Keith Halliwell, who contributes to the document.

The main elements are:
- inform and educate young people about drugs
- help drug misusing offenders to tackle their drug problems and thereby reduce the levels of crime
- increase the participation of drug misusers, including prisoners, in drug treatment programmes
- reduce the availability of drugs

Each element of the strategy relies on statutory, voluntary and private sectors working in partnership, and for there to be a rigorous assessment of the effectiveness of implementing the strategy using research, audit and consultation.

Further reading:
Farrell, M. and Strang, J. (1998) Britain's new strategy for tackling drugs misuse shows a welcome emphasis on evidence. *British Medical Journal* 316(142) 1399-400

Department of Health (1998) *Modernising mental health services: safe, sound and supportive.* London: Department of Health

Summary: as part of the government's modernisation of the NHS, this reviews the current state of mental health, noting the high level of suicide in young people as well as the link between severe mental illness and violence. Proposals for improvement include:

- creating a needs-led service that will also protect the public
- full access to service including a 24-hour crisis service
- supporting families and carers as well as patients
- establishing integrated care by working with agencies in education, housing and employment
- under guidance from NICE, ensuring service is efficient and cost effective

The government plans to commit £700 million to improvements over three years. These will include the provision of extra beds and better outreach services. Primary care groups will work closely with specialist teams to integrate planning and delivery. Secure hospitals to be improved. Performance will be monitored through new assessment frameworks for health and social care and a new national service framework for mental health will determine service models and standards.

Further reading:
Jackson, Catherine (1999) Gold blend. *Mental Health Care* 2(6) 190-1
McFadyen, J.A. (1999) Modernising mental health services: the right ACT for the wrong reason? *British Journal of Health Care Management* 5(1) 28-34
Scott, Helen (1998) Review of mental health law must be courageous. *British Journal of Nursing* 7(19) 1138

Department of Health (1998) *Mental Health Act 1983: memorandum on parts I to IV, VIII and X.* London: The Stationery Office

Summary: this is intended as guidance for mental health workers on implementing the 1983 Act. It covers the sections which deal with patient admission, supervised discharge, remand, consent to treatment and detention under the Act. It also defines and clarifies some of the terms used in the Act and is recommended to be read in conjunction with the new *Code of practice (1999).*

Royal College of Nursing (1999) *RCN mental health nursing strategy.* London: RCN

Summary: the RCN's reponse to *Modernising mental health services (1998)* and other current circumstances affecting mental health. The responses involve lobbying for improvements, opening dialogue with agencies such as the Royal College of Psychiatrists, UKCC, Department of Health and so on and setting guidelines for good practice.

All respond to questions dealing with clinical interventions, safety for staff and the public, safety for patients, admissions and bed issues, culture and ethnicity, human resources and research and practice development.

Department of Health (1999) *Code of practice: Mental Health Act 1983.* London: The Stationery Office

Summary: for use by all health professionals in the field of mental health as well as the police and social services. Updating the 1993 *Code of practice*, this code gives guidance on how the 1983 Act should be applied in the light of new law and terminology. It highlights the rights of individuals under the *European Convention on Human Rights (1978)* and encourages the use of the new Care Programme Approach in mental health services. The code also stresses the importance of communication with patients, confidentiality and giving information to patients and their relatives.

Further reading:
Bluglass, Robert (1983) *A guide to the Mental Health Act 1983.* Edinburgh: Churchill Livingstone
Dolan, Bridget and Powell, Debra (2001) *The point of law: the Mental Health Act explained.* London: The Stationery Office

Department of Health (1999) *Safer services: national confidential inquiry into suicide and homicide by people with mental illness.* (chair Louis Appleby) London: Department of Health

Summary: report commissioned to collect data on mental health patients in England and Wales who have committed suicide or homicide, and to recommend health policy to reduce the risks of such incidents in the future. The findings consider factors such as: last contact with mental health services; prevention; in-patient and post-discharge; homelessness; non-compliance with treatment; previous violent offences; drug and alcohol misuse and dependence and ethnic groups. Key findings include:

- 24% of suicide cases were in contact with mental health services during the previous year, and the inquiry believes that many are not inevitable but preventable through improved services to reduce risk
- 8% of convicted homicides were in contact with mental health services in the previous year and 14% at some time, mostly for substance dependence or personality disorder rather than mental illness, but these cases were less preventable than the suicides
- the majority of homicides have a history of violence and substance misuse

Among the recommendations for improving mental health services are:
- regular staff training concentrating on high risk groups and substance misuse
- to ensure that all relevant information reaches every agency involved, streamlined documentation in the form of "patient passports" that will record mental health history and previous violent offences
- new "atypical" drug treatment to be used where possible to reduce risk of side effects; non-compliance information to be better documented

- health authorities to have a better policy for those who are disengaged from services, including methods of outreach
- measures to prevent in-patient suicides such as increased monitoring and the removal of structures which could be used for hanging
- better follow-up after discharge in at-risk cases, giving help with finding accommodation
- use of mental health legislation in cases of high risk or non-compliance
- highest level of care under the care programme approach (CPA)

Finally, the Committee believes that the Department of Health should re-evaluate the system of local inquiries into cases: the present system often engenders a "culture of blame" against staff and therefore do not always produce worthwhile results.

Standing Nursing and Midwifery Advisory Committee (1999) *Mental health nursing: "addressing acute concerns"*. (chair Tony Bell) London: Department of Health

Summary: with the shift from hospital to community care in recent years, the report finds that in spite of the severity of patients' illnesses and the complexity of their needs, acute mental health care has deteriorated. Issues include:

- staffing: there is poor clinical leadership, inadequate education and training, insufficient staff numbers with problems of recruitment and retention, and a lack of support from other professional groups
- safety: women and other vulnerable groups have little privacy and are vulnerable to assault and sexual abuse; violence and aggression is also a problem for staff
- race: the needs of minority groups are not recognised and staff themselves are subject to racial discrimination
- health policy: mental health nurses are not practicing evidence-based care or involving users and carers in planning, practising and evaluating care

Recommendations are directed at various agencies and include:

- NHS executive to develop evidence-based guidelines for acute mental health care
- Chief Nursing Officers to promote clinical leadership and the recognition of acute care as a worthwhile career
- education: service and education providers to collaborate to produce programmes in: acute care, assessment, risk assessment, involving users, the management of violence, and interventions including medication and therapies
- research is needed to improve the evidence base in acute care, the therapeutic culture and liaison nursing
- employers to develop formal methods of patient assessment; involve users and carers; make better use of liaison nurses in casualty departments; develop clinical leadership; promote nurse consultant posts; promote staff and patient safety; consider needs of minority groups and racial discrimination within staffing structures

Department of Health (1999) *National service framework for mental health: modern standards and service models.* London: Department of Health

Summary: building on the principles outlined in *Modernising mental health services (1998)*, this framework establishes standards and models of service delivery. For the first time, milestones and performance indicators are set, against which progress can be measured. Aimed at the adult population to age sixtyfive, the framework covers five areas:

- mental health promotion
- primary care
- access to services
- effective care for those with severe mental illness, and the prevention of suicide
- support for carers

Further reading:
Tyrer, P. (1999) The national service framework: a scaffold for mental health. *British Medical Journal* 319(7216) 1017-8
Thornicroft, G. (2000) National service framework for mental health. *Psychiatric Bulletin* 24(6) 203-6

Faculty of Health, University of Central Lancashire (1999) *Nursing in secure environments.* London: United Kingdom Central Council for Nursing, Midwifery and Health Visiting

Summary: a commissioned study that aims to present a picture of what is expected of nurses in secure environments in order to create an action plan. The study looked at nursing in secure hospitals and in prisons where many issues arise with their responsibility for maintaining security as well as giving care. The study also found that working in 'closed' institutions led to difficulties with developing practice and sustaining relationships. Recommendations cover education, the evidence base, standards and competencies, clinical supervision, managing violence and challenging behaviour as well as cultural and gender issues.

Further reading:
Polczyk-Przbyla, M. and Gournay, Kevin (1999) Psychiatric nursing in prison: the state of the art? *Journal of Advanced Nursing* 30(4) 893-900

Audit Commission (2000) *Forget me not: mental health services for older people.* London: Audit Commission (see Chapter 6. Older People)

Ward, M. et al (2000) *The nursing, midwifery and health visiting contribution to the continuing care of people with mental health problems.* London: United Kingdom Central Council for Nursing, Midwifery and Health Visiting

Summary: a review recommending improvements in education and work practices of mental health practitioners, especially in primary care. Data was collected via focus groups, questionnaires and a literature review. Findings and recommendations are grouped as follows:

- training: the review found a lack of research awareness and skills and a concern from non-mental health nurses about their own lack of knowledge. There should be training for research methods via university modules and critical appraisal skills programmes; also an element of mental health training for nurses in all branches
- case management: the review found a lack of information in specialist areas such as child and adolescent mental health with a lack of motivation to undertake higher education programmes. The report recommends investigating information provision in specialist areas
- care delivery: the review found a lack of communication between NHS trusts and a lack of user involvement in development and evaluation of services.
- the way forward: the report found a lack of published work by practitioners, a lack of professional development and the funding to support it, also Trusts are failing to share good practice and innovation. There should be greater encouragement to publish research and other work; Trusts should encourage staff development and there should be a formal network for the exchange of ideas
- leadership: the review found a lack of sufficient clinical supervision and that practitioners were unable to introduce new working practices owing to continuous organisational change. Supervision and mentorship to be provided for all staff and innovative service development to be encouraged

Mental Health Foundation (2000) *Strategies for living: a report of user-led research into people's strategies for living with mental distress.* London: MHF

Summary: 76 people were interviewed to find out how they coped when they suffered mental illness or distress: what treatments were helpful eg medication and 'talking therapies', and what strategies they used they used to help themselves eg exercise, creative activities. This was a three year study whose aims were to help other sufferers by publicising these strategies, promoting a holistic approach to mental health care, and encouraging user-led research in mental health. Participants were chosen on the basis of experience of different therapies, ethnic origin, age and geographic location, with an almost equal ratio of men to women. Also included were people with 'severe mental health problems'. As regards treatments and strategies for coping, variety seems to be key but the study also gives valuable insight into users' perceptions of mental health services as well as the effect of living with the stigma of mental illness.

Department of Health (2000) *Reforming the Mental Health Act. Part 1: the new legal framework (cm5016-I); part 2: high risk patients (cm5016-II)* London: The Stationery Office

Summary: this two-part white paper applies to mental health care in England only. *Part 1: the new legal framework* deals with the detention of the small minority of people with a mental illness who present a risk to themselves and others. A new framework is needed effectively to detain patients without contravening the *Human Rights Act 1998.*

- established criteria must be met before detention in each case, the decision to detain made by three mental health professionals
- the initial period of detention is to be no more than 28 days before being assessed by the Mental Health Tribunal who may authorise a further six or twelve months during which a specific care plan must be followed
- in some cases compulsory powers may be applied to patients cared for in the community: for instance in administering medication or attending day care
- rights and safeguards: patients and their relatives are to be informed of the law under which they are being treated; they may request a review of the Mental Health Tribunal Order; they must have the opportunity to take free legal and advocacy advice; they may be involved in treatment plans when social and cultural backgrounds should be considered
- a specialist in child mental health must be involved in treatment plans for children
- a new Commission for Mental Health will protect patients' interests, oversee the use of legislation, ensure training needs are met and must be consulted when patients are unable to give consent to treatment and when ECT and psychosurgery are recommended as treatments

Part 2: high risk patients sets policy for high risk patients in the light of Government's priority to protect the safety of the public. It details assessment criteria and care of detainees. Two categories are named: those who present a danger to themselves and those who are a danger to others.

- health and social care workers to act in cooperation with agencies such as the police, the courts and prison and probation services, acting in consideration of legislation such as the *Criminal Justice Act 2000*
- care plans to emphasise therapeutic treatment as well as detention
- for the dangerous and severely personality disordered (DSPD) group, pilot schemes run in 2001 may result in new powers for mental health practitioners, and lead to the creation of specific accommodation in prisons, hospitals and community hostels. A specialist team will decide whether DSPD status applies and where there is a criminal conviction, courts can choose between a prison sentence, a care and treatment order, a restriction order or a hospital and limitation direction
- there will be more sharing of information between health and social care and law enforcement services, particularly in cases of violent and sexual crimes. Relevant departments to be alerted when a patient or offender leaves detention or moves between NHS and prison services
- the Mental Health Tribunals can set conditions on a patient's discharge and in some cases, recall them to detention

Further reading:
Criminal Justice & Court Services Act 2000: chapter 43. London: The Stationery Office
Dimond, B. (2001) Reform of mental health law must not be rushed.
British Journal of Nursing 10(2) 69
Donnelly, L. (2001) A tough nut to crack. *Health Service Journal* 111(5737) 11-12
Grounds, A. (2001) Reforming the Mental Health Act.
British Journal of Psychiatry 179 387-9
Jackson, C. (2001) Law and disordered.
Mental Health and Learning Disabilities Care 4(6) 184-5

Supplementary Reading

Braisby, D. et al (1988) *Changing futures: housing and support services for people discharged from psychiatric hospitals (project paper 76).* London: King's Fund

Charlwood, P. et al (eds) (1999) *Health outcome indicators: severe mental illness: report of a working group to the Department of Health.* Oxford: National Centre for Health Outcomes Development

Clinical Standards Advisory Group (1995) *Schizophrenia: volume 2: protocol for assessing services for people with a severe mental illness.* London: HMSO

Department of Health (1992) *Review of health and social services for mentally disordered offenders and others requiring similar services (cm2088).* (chair J.L. Reed) London: HMSO

Department of Health (1996) *Building bridges: a guide to arrangements for inter-agency working for the care and protection of severely mentally ill people: the health of the nation.* London: HMSO

Echlin, R. (1995) *Partners in change: care planning in mental health services.* London: King's Fund

Faulkener, A. Field, V. and Muijen, M. (1994) *A survey of adult mental health services.* London: The Sainsbury Centre for Mental Health

Lord Chancellor's Department (1999) *Making decisions: the government's proposals for making decisions on behalf of mentally incapacitated adults: a report issued in the light of the consultation paper "Who decides" (1997).* London: The Stationery Office

McCulloch, A. Warner, L. and Villeneau, L. (2000) *Taking your partners: using opportunities for inter-agency partnership in mental health.* London: Sainsbury Centre for Mental Health

Mental Health Foundation (1994) *Creating community care: report of the Mental Health Foundation inquiry into community care of people with severe mental illness.* London: Mental Health Foundation

Mental Health Foundation (2000) *Pull yourself together!: a survey of the stigma and discrimination faced by people who experience mental distress.* London: MHF

NHS Advisory Service (1995) *People who are homeless.* London: HMSO

NHS Executive (1996) *NHS psychotherapy services in England: a review of strategic policy.* London: Department of Health

NHS Executive (1996) *24-hour nursed care for people with severe and enduring mental illness.* London: Department of Health

Royal College of Psychiatrists (1996) *Report of the confidential inquiry into homicides and suicides by mentally ill people.* (chair W.D.Boyd) London: RCP

Sainsbury Centre for Mental Health (1998) *Acute problems: a survey of the quality of care in acute psychiatric wards.* London: The Sainsbury Centre for Mental Health

10 Learning Disabilities

Department of Health (1991) *Caring for people: community care in the next decade and beyond - mental handicap nursing.* (chair C. Cullen) London: HMSO

Summary: recommendations of the nursing profession for mental handicap services in relation to community care policy, concentrating on skills and qualifications, and cooperation with the rest of the health care team in providing services. Specific recommendations made to the Department of Health and the statutory bodies concerning development of services and education and training of staff, and collaboration with social services and the independent sector.

Further reading:
Allen, M.(1991) Cullen in a clear vision for the future...mentally handicapped nursing. *Nursing (London)* 4(29) 3
Crawford, M. (1991) New report recognises value of mental handicap nurses...Cullen report. *Nursing (London)* 4(29) 4-5

Department of Health (1995) *Health of the nation: a strategy for people with learning disabilities.* London: HMSO

Summary: this booklet is aimed at health commissioners. The first section looks at improving general health, carers, and cooperation between different service providers. Subsequent three sections examine health promotion, health surveillance and health care. Finally there are sections on the five key target areas of the Health of the Nation - heart disease, cancer, HIV and sexual health, accidents, mental illness - and their implementation in the specific context of learning disabilities services.

Department of Health (1995) *Learning disability: meeting needs through targeting skills.* London: HMSO

Summary: this guide is a result of the Learning Disability Nursing Project, and is aimed at commissioners and providers of services, GP fundholders, NHS trusts and the independent sector. The introduction gives an overview of the learning disability population and services provided, outlines key points for purchasers, and informs about the role and contribution of learning disability nurses and the settings in which they work. The rest of the document consists of fourteen case studies in five categories: child health, meeting health needs, independent sector, local authority social services, and challenging behaviour.

Kay, B. Rose, S. and Turnbull, J. (1995) *Continuing the commitment: the report of the Learning Disability Nursing Project.* London: HMSO

Summary: the Learning Disability Nursing Project was set up to examine the skills and role of learning disability nurses, and examples of best practice. This report informs purchasers and providers on service needs in the context of those key areas of the Project. There is a section on learning disability nurses' key knowledge and skills followed by recommendations for nurses, for education, for nursing organisations and for the Department of Health.

Further reading:
Francis, R. (1995) It's good to talk...Learning Disability Nursing Project. *Nursing Standard* 10(4 - No Limits supplement) 54
Jukes, M. (1995) Enhancing service provision for people with learning disabilities. *British Journal of Nursing* 4(11) 614-615
Kay, B. (1995) Grasping the nettle in learning disabilities nursing. *British Journal of Nursing* 4(2 - British Journal of Learning Disability Nursing supplement) 96-98
Lawrie, K. (1995) Better health care for people with learning disabilities. *Nursing Times* 91(19) 32-34
Rose, K. and Kay, B. (1995) Significant skills...learning disability nursing project. *Nursing Times* 91(36) 63-64

Disability Discrimination Act 1995: chapter 50. London: HMSO

Summary: this Act makes it unlawful to discriminate against disabled people in employment, goods and services, premises and accommodation, education, and transport, providing mechanisms for complaint and penalties for non-compliance.

- employment: this includes applications for work, conditions and terms of employment, employers' obligation to provide for the needs of disabled employees (with exemption for small businesses)
- goods and services: these include public places, hotels, information services, banking and insurance services and professional and trade services
- premises and accommodation: this includes providing equal access to living accommodation and work premises
- education: looks and both further and higher education and includes amendments to the *Education Act 1993: chapter 62* and the *Further and Higher Education Act 1992: chapter 13*
- this looks at adjustments to vehicles with detailed points on taxis, public service vehicles and rail services

The Act also provides for the establishment of a National Disability Council whose role is to advise the Secretary of State, issue codes of practice, gather information and give advice. The Act came into force in 1997

Further reading:
Bartram, M. (1997) Sign up to serve. *Nursing Management* 3(8) 12-13
Clements, Luke (1998) Acts of weakness. *Community Care* 8.1.1998 26-7
Memel, David and Francis, Kate (2000) The Disability Discrimination Act: an opportunity more than threat. *British Journal of General Practice* 50(461) 950-51
Stanton, B. (1997) The Disability Discrimination Act in practice. *British Journal of Health Care Management* 3(2) 106-8

Mental Health Foundation (1996) *Building expectations: opportunities and services for people with a learning disability.* London: Mental Health Foundation

Summary: many learning disabled people live in the community, but do not always get the recognition of their needs and their potential to contribute to society. This report encourages that recognition and makes recommendations about services and opportunities. Key aspects of the report include recommending new government funding for both services and staff training, and cooperation between health and social services. Other areas which are given attention include independent living, training and employment, recreation activities, and advocacy. The appointment of care managers and keyworkers to assess the needs of those with learning disabilities in all these areas, and to arrange services, is strongly recommended.

Further reading:
Leifer, D. (1996) Take time to explain. *Nursing Standard* 11(2) 14
McMillan, I. (1996) Special needs cry out for special care. *Nursing Times* 92(39) 19
Richardson, A. (1996) A fitting response. *Health Service Journal* 106(5527) 29

NHS Executive (1998) *Signposts for success in commissioning and providing health services for people with learning disabilities.* London: Department of Health

Summary: describes the role of the NHS and local authority social services in the provision of learning disability services, both now and in their future roles. The document provides guidelines for health service commissioners and providers and gives recommendations for good practice in specific areas such as children, and also epilepsy and other physical disabilities. The end of the document contains eleven pages of further reading and addresses of useful organisations.

Further reading:
Parrish, A. (1998) Exploring the NHS executive document 'Signposts for success'. *British Journal of Nursing* 7(8) 478-80
Thomas, D. (1998) Signposting the way forward. *Mental Health Care* 1(7) 224

UKCC (1998) *Guidelines for mental health and learning disability nursing.* London: UKCC

Summary: the UKCC's guidelines on areas such as confidentiality, ethical issues and interdisciplinary work. The booklet also emphasises the importance of evidence-based practice and suggests other relevant publications and guidelines.

Department of Health (1999) *Facing the facts: services for people with learning difficulties: a policy impact study of social care and health studies.* London: The Stationery Office

Summary: this report is the result of a survey carried out in 1998/9 in twenty four local authorities and partner health authorities. Findings are that progress has been made since 1992 when guidance on people with learning difficulties was issued to health and social services. They include observations on overall vision and change, accommodation and care, employment and day services, health services, protection from abuse, commissioning of services, expenditure, care management and performance management. However a considerable amount still needs to be done: between the authorities service is inconsistent and of variable quality. The report concludes that whilst examples of good practice can be found in most areas, these are usually on a small scale and national objectives and achievement targets are needed.

Disability Rights Commission Act 1999: chapter 17.
London: The Stationery Office

Summary: the Act arises from a consultation paper: *Promoting disabled people's rights (1998)*. The Act provides for a Disability Rights Commission with the following powers:
- to work on the elimination of discrimination against disabled people
- to promote equal opportunities
- improve the treatment of disabled people
- to review the *Disability Discrimination Act 1995*
- to undertake formal investigations
- offer advice and support to disabled people, employers and service providers
- promote the rights of disabled people

Further reading:
Department of Health (1998) *Promoting disabled people's rights: creating a Disability Rights Commission fit for the C21st (cm3977)*. London: The Stationery Office
Jackson, C. (2000) Right on our side.
Mental Health and Learning Disabilities Care 4(1) 6-8
Revans, L. (2000) Commission seeks to add to its remit. *Community Care* 14.9.2000 12

Department of Health (2001) *Valuing people: a new strategy for learning disabilities for the 21st century (cm5086)*. London: Department of Health

Summary: the first white paper to be published in learning disabilities for thirty years. The paper takes a broad approach, looking at people from childhood to old age, with proposals involving every government agency: housing, health and social care, education etc.

The current situation: problems boil down to issues of social exclusion, inconsistency in provision of services that are unresponsive to need, poor management, insufficient qualified staff and inadequate connexions between the various agencies.

The ten proposals are based on four principles:
- civil rights
- independence
- choice
- inclusion

The proposals include:
- an integrated, interagency approach to services for children with disabilities

- a National Information Centre
- accommodation: choice in housing and accommodation in the community for those who still remain in long-term hospitals
- a Health Action Plan for every disabled person
- a programme to modernise day services
- to increase employment opportunities
- person-centred planning: a new approach to planning care and services for individuals
- local councils to take lead responsibility in coordinating local services

Further reading:
Burns, J. (2001) Welcome to the 21st century. *Open Mind* Nov/Dec 2001 12-3
Community Living (2001) 14(4 supplement) whole issue
Gates, B. (2001) Valuing people: long awaited strategy for people with learning disabilities for the 21st century in England. *J of Learning Disabilities* 5(3) 203-7

Supplementary Reading

Audit Commission (1987) *Community care: developing services for people with a mental handicap. (Occasional paper number 4).* London: HMSO

Blunden, R. and Allen, D. (1987) *Facing the challenge: an ordinary life for people with learning difficulties and challenging behaviour.* London: King's Fund

Clifton, M. (1993) *Learning disabilities and challenging behaviour.* London: ENB

Cox, C. and Pearson, M. (1995) *Made to care: the case for residential and village communities for people with a mental handicap.* London: The Rannoch Trust

Elliott-Cannon, C. (1995) *Building a partnership: co-operation to promote shared learning in the field of learning disability.* London: ENB/CCETSW

Emerson, E. (1994) *Moving out: the impact of relocation from hospital to community on the quality of life of people with learning disabilities.* London: HMSO

Emerson, E. et al (1996) *Residential provision for people with learning disabilities: summary report.* Manchester: University of Manchester

Kay, B. et al (1996) *Learning disability nursing project resource package.* London: HMSO

McIntosh, B. (ed)(1998) *Days of change: a practical guide to developing better day opportunities with people with learning difficulties.* London: Kings Fund

Norman, I.J. et al (1996) *The changing educational needs of mental health and learning disability nurses.* London: ENB

Redfern, S. (1996) *An investigation into the changing pre- and post-registration educational needs of mental health and learning disability nurses.* London: ENB

Services for people with learning disabilities and challenging behaviour or mental health problems: report of a project group (1993). (chair J. L. Mansell) London: HMSO

Taylor, J. (1986) *Mental handicap: partnership in the community?* London: Office of Health Economics and Mencap

Wertheimer, A. (1996) *Changing days: developing new daytime opportunities for people who have learning difficulties.* London: Kings Fund

Whittaker, A. et al (1991) *Service evaluation by people with learning difficulties.* London: King's Fund

Applying for Jobs

Suggested Reading

BMJ Classified (1996) *Career focus: information that helps develop careers.* London: BMJ Publishing Group

Chambers, R. et al (2000) *Opportunities and options in medical careers.* Abingdon: Radcliffe Medical Press

Freeman, A.E.L. and Wozniak, E.R. (2001) Preparing for consultant interview: advice from a regional advisor. *Current Paediatrics* 11(6) 470-4

Hill, B. (2000) In the hot seat. *Nursing Standard* 14(50) 59

Howard, S. (1999) *Creating a successful CV.* London: Dorling Kindersley

Little Tim (1996) *Power CVs and interview letters that really work.* Richmond: Langley Publishing

MacCallum, E. (2001) The first step to finding your first job. *Mental Health Practice* 4(6) 30-1

McKenzie, S. (2001) Writing your curriculum vitae. *Hospital Medicine* 62(9) 568-70

Marino, K. (2000) *Resumes for the healthcare professional.-2e* Chichester: John Wiley

Mumford, C.J. (2000) *Medical job interview: secrets for success.* Oxford: Blackwell

Robotham, M. (2001) How to make yourself just the job. *Nursing Times* 97(22) 24-5

Robotham, M. (2001) How to shine at the interview. *Nursing Times* 97(22) 26-7

Organisations

BRITISH ASSOCIATION OF SOCIAL WORKERS
16 Kent St, BIRMINGHAM B5 6RD
☎ 0121 622 3911
www.basw.co.uk
Purpose: "...the largest association representing social work and social workers in the UK...here to help, support, advise and campaign..."

BRITISH MEDICAL ASSOCIATION
BMA House, Tavistock Square, LONDON WC1H 9JP
☎ 020 7387 4499
www.bma.org.uk
Purpose: "We put the profession's democratically reached views to national administrations and many other influential bodies. We are an independent trade union officially recognised by government and the pay review bodies for negotiation on doctors' pay and conditions."

COMMUNITY AND DISTRICT NURSING ASSOCIATION
Westel House, 32-8 Uxbridge Rd, LONDON W5 2BS
☎ 020 8280 5342
www.cdna.tvu.ac.uk
Purpose: "...to provide a quality industrial relations and professional service... and to lead and influence policy making decisions on professional issues relating to health care in the community...."

COMMUNITY PRACTITIONER AND HEALTH VISITORS' ASSOCIATION
(was Health Visitors' Association)
50 Southwark Street, London, SE1 1UN
☎ 020 7717 4000
www.msf.org.uk/cphva.html
Purpose: "a profesional organisation (and trade union)... for all nurse members in the primary health care team...with a strong focus on health promotion, preventive health care and the broad issues around public health."

DEPARTMENT OF HEALTH
Richmond House, 79 Whitehall, London, SW1A 2NS
for general enquiries ☎ 020 7210 4850 (open 9am – 5pm)
www.doh.gov.uk

DEPARTMENT FOR WORK AND PENSIONS
(was Dept of Social Security)
Correspondence Unit, Room 540, The Adelphi, 1-11 John Adam St, LONDON WC2N 6HT
☎ 020 7712 2171
www.dwp.gov.uk

GENERAL MEDICAL COUNCIL
178 Great Portland St, LONDON W1W 5JE
☎ 020 7580 7642
www.gmc-uk.org

Purpose: "a charity... whose purpose is the protection, promotion and maintenance of the health and safety of the community. We have strong and effective legal powers designed to maintain the standards the public have the right to expect of doctors. We are not here to protect the medical profession...Our job is to protect patients"

GENERAL SOCIAL CARE COUNCIL
Goldings House, 2 Hay's Lane, LONDON SE1 2HB
☎ 020 7397 5100
www.doh.gov.uk/gscc

Purpose: established in October 2001, the GSCC regulates social care workers. It sets codes of conduct and practice; regulates social work education and training and establishes a register of social care workers.

HEALTH PROFESSIONS COUNCIL
Park House, 184 Kennington Park Road, LONDON SE11 4BU
☎ 020 7582 0866
www.hpcuk.org

Purpose: the HPC replaces the Council for Professions Supplementary to Medicine. It has been set up to regulate 12 healthcare professions – such as chiropodists, speech therapists, physiotherapists etc – with a view to safeguarding the health and wellbeing of patients and ensuring the professions are qualified and competent.

JOSEPH ROWNTREE FOUNDATION
The Homestead, 40 Water End, YORK YO30 6WP
☎ 01904 629241
www.jrf.org.uk

Purpose: an independent social policy research and development charity; supports a wide programme of research and development projects in housing, social care and social policy.

KING'S FUND
11-13 Cavendish Square, London W1G 0AN
☎ 020 7307 2400
www.kingsfund.org.uk

Purpose: "... to stimulate and disseminate good practice and innovation in health and related services....make an independent and influential, contribution to the development of health policy nationally and internationally."

NATIONAL INSTITUTE FOR SOCIAL WORK
5 Tavistock Place
LONDON WC1H 9SN
☎ 020 7387 9681
www.nisw.org.uk

Purpose: established in 1961, the Institute provides staff training, research and specialist library resources for the personal social services, "...actively raising standards and promoting good practice in the public, independent and voluntary sectors".

NURSING AND MIDWIFERY COUNCIL
23 Portland Place, LONDON W1B 1PZ
☎ 020 7637 7181
www.nmc-uk.org

Purpose: replacing the ENB and UKCC, from 1.4.02 the NMC regulates nursing, midwifery and health visiting. It maintains a register of nurses midwives and health visitors, sets standards for their education, practice and conduct, provides advice and considers allegations of misconduct or unfitness to practice.

THE QUEEN'S NURSING INSTITUTE
3 Albemarle Way, London, EC1V 4RQ
☎ 020 7490 4227
www.qni.org.uk

Purpose: "... promotes the highest standards of nursing in the community... to encourage the best possible community health care and public health"

ROYAL COLLEGE OF MIDWIVES - RCM
15 Mansfield Street, London, W1G 9NH
☎ 020 7312 3535
www.rcm.org.uk

Purpose: "...exists to protect and advance the interests of midwives/midwifery... supplying professional/educational services,...industrial relations advice, support and information."

ROYAL COLLEGE OF NURSING - RCN
20 Cavendish Square, London, W1G 0RN
☎ 0845 772 6100
www.rcn.org.uk

Purpose: a trade union that serves its 303,000+ members in professional matters, labour relations and education.

WORLD HEALTH ORGANIZATION
Avenue Appia 20, 1211 GENEVA 27, Switzerland
☎ 004122 791 2111
www.who.int

Websites

Audit Commission	www.audit-commission.gov.uk
BMA	www.bma.org.uk
CCTA Government Information Service	www.open.gov.uk
Commission for Health Improvement	www.chi.nhs.uk
Department of Health	www.doh.gov.uk
Department of Work and Pensions	www.dwp.gov.uk
Electronic Library for Social Care	www.elsc.org.uk
ENB	www.enb.org.uk
General Medical Council	www.gmc-uk.org
General Social Care Council	www.doh.gov.uk/gscc
Health Professions Council	www.hpcuk.org
King's Fund	www.kingsfund.org.uk/
MIDIRS	www.midirs.org.uk
National Electronic Library for Health	www.nelh.nhs.uk
National Institue for Social Work	www.nisw.org.uk
Nursing and Midwifery Council	www.nmc-uk.org
Official Publications	www.official-documents.co.uk
OMNI (medical gateway)	www.omni.ac.uk
Royal College of Midwives	www.rcm.org.uk
Royal College of Nursing	www.rcn.org.uk
Sainsbury Centre for Mental Health	www.sainsburycentre.org.uk
SCHARR	www.shef.ac.uk/uni/academic/R-Z/scharr
SOSIG (social science gateway)	www.sosig.ac.uk
WHO	www.who.org

Alphabetical Index

title	page
Accountable care: developing the GSCC.	60
The Acheson report	51
Adopting changes.	105
Adoption: a new approach.	106
The Allitt inquiry (Clothier report)	94
The Appleby report	121
The Baker report	62
The Bell report	122
Better care, higher standards	59
Better off in the community? The care of people who are seriously mentally ill	116
Breaking the boundaries	74
Brief encounters: getting the best from temporary nursing staff	29
A bridge to the future	101
Bridging the gaps	93
Bringing Britain together: a national strategy for neighbourhood renewal	43
Building a safer NHS for patients	67
Building bridges	117
Building expectations: opportunities and services for people with a learning disability	129
The Butterworth report	115
The Caldicott report	56
The Calman report	19
The care of sick children	95
Care Standards Act 2000	45
Carers (Recognition and Services) Act 1995	38
Caring about carers: a national strategy for carers	44
Caring for people: community care in the next decade and beyond	35
Caring for people (Cullen report)	127
The challenges for nursing and midwifery in the 21st century: the Heathrow debate	20

title	page
Change here! Managing change to improve local services	47
Changing childbirth	109
Child and adolescent mental health services (Health Committee 4th report)	99
Child health in the community	96
Child protection: guidance for senior nurses, health visitors and midwives	92
Children Act 1989	91
The Children Act 1989: what every nurse, midwife and health visitor needs to know	93
Children first: a study of hospital services	93
Children (Leaving Care) Act 2000	105
Choice and opportunity: primary care: the future	38
The Clark report	84
The Clothier report	94
Code of practice: Mental Health Act 1983	121
The coming of age: improving care services for older people	83
Commissioning mental health services	117
Community care: agenda for action (Griffiths report)	34
Community health care for elderly people (Clark report)	84
Comprehensive critical care	25
A consultation on a strategy for nursing, midwifery and health visiting	22
The consumer's view: elderly people and community health services	81
Continuing the commitment: the report of the learning disability nursing project	127
Cover story: the use of locum doctors in NHS trusts	24
The Crown report	25

title	page
The Cullen report	127
The Cumberledge report (1986)	33
The Cumberledge report (1993)	109
The Dearing report	73
Developing partnerships in mental health	118
Developing quality to protect children	106
Developing roles of nurses in clinical child health	96
Developments in midwifery education and practice: a progress report	110
Disability Discrimination Act 1995	128
Disability Rights Commission Act 1999	130
The doctors' tale	20
The Donaldson report	61
Educating and training the future health professional workforce for England	78
Emergency services for children and young people	97
Establishing the new Nursing and Midwifery Council	66
Excellence, not excuses	46
Facing the facts	129
A fair deal for older people	87
Finding a place: a review of mental health services for adults	116
First assessment: a review of district nursing services in England and Wales	43
First class delivery: improving maternity services in England and Wales	112
A first class service: quality in the new NHS	57
Fitness for practice (The Peach report)	76
Forget me not	87
Fully equipped	86
Future imperfect	47
The future of professional practice	72
Getting ahead of the curve	54
The Griffiths report	34

title	page
Guidelines for mental health and learning disability nursing	129
Half a century of promises	82
Harold Shipman's clinical practice (the Baker report)	62
The Health Act 1999	24
The health of the nation	49
The health of the nation: handbook on child and adolescent mental health	94
The health of the nation key area handbook: mental illness	115
The health of the nation: strategy for people with learning disabilities	127
A health service of all the talents	77
Health services for children and young people	96
Health services for children and young people in the community (3rd report)	98
Healthcare futures 2010	75
The Heathrow debate	20
Hidden talents	77
Higher education in the learning society (Dearing report)	73
A higher level of practice	25
High hopes: making housing and community care work	40
Home alone: the role of housing in community care	39
Homeward bound: a new course for community health	37
Hospital services for children and young people (Health Committee 5th report)	100
Human Rights Act 1998	58
The Hutton report	28
Ignored and invisible?	41
Independent inquiry into inequalities in health (Acheson report)	51
Informal carers	41
Information for social care	67
The interface between junior doctors and nurses (Calman report)	19
In the public interest: developing a strategy for public participation in the NHS	57
Into the 90s	37

title	page
JM Consulting report	23
Just for the day	92
The Kennedy report	64
The last straw: explaining the NHS nursing shortage	26
Lecturer practitioner roles in England	73
Learning disability: meeting needs through targeting skills	127
Learning the lessons	117
Leaving hospital: elderly people and their discharge to community care	81
The McIntosh report	97
Making a reality of community care	33
Making it happen	50
Making the change: a strategy for the professions in healthcare science	29
Maternity services (Winterton report)	109
Me, survive out there?	104
Meeting the challenge: a strategy for allied health professionals	26
Mental Health Act 1983	115
Mental Health Act 1983: memorandum on parts I-IV, VIII and X	120
Mental health nursing: addressing acute concerns (the Bell report)	122
Mental Health (Patients in the Community) Act 1995	116
Midwifery educational resource pack: the challenge of *Changing childbirth*	111
Midwifery: delivering our future (Norman report)	112
Modernising mental health services: safe, sound and supportive	120
Modernising social services	41
The named nurse, midwife and health visitor	19
NAWCH quality review	91
NHS and Community Care Act 1990	17
The NHS: a service with ambitions	21
The NHS plan: a plan for investment, a plan for reform	27

title	page
The NHS plan: the Government's response to the Royal Commission on Long Term Care	86
NHS (Primary Care) Act 1997	39
NHS Reform and Health Care Professions Bill 2001	31
National service framework for mental health: modern standards and service models	123
National service framework for older people	88
National strategy for sexual health and HIV	53
National taskforce on violence against social care staff	30
The national visit	118
Neighbourhood nursing: a focus for care (Cumberledge report)	33
New life for health (the Hutton report)	28
The new NHS: modern, dependable	21
A new partnership for care in old age	83
New world, new opportunities	37
Nine to thirteen: the forgotten years?	105
The Norman report	112
Not because they are old	85
Nurses, Midwives and Health Visitors Act 1992	18
Nurses, Midwives and Health Visitors Act 1997	22
Nursing education: implementation of Project 2000 in England	72
Nursing in secure environments	123
Nursing in the community (Roy report)	36
The nursing contribution to the continuing care of people with mental health problems	123
Old habits die hard	88
Omnibus survey	89
Opportunity for all: tackling poverty and social exclusion	44
An organisation with a memory	61
Our healthier nation: a contract for health	50

title	page
Paediatric intensive care: a framework for the future	100
Partnership in action	42
The patient's charter	55
The patients charter and you. [rev ed]	55
The patient's charter: maternity services	110
The patient's charter: mental health services	117
The patient's charter: services for children and young people	95
The Peach report	76
People like us	101
Poverty and social exclusion in Britain	46
Preparation of supervisors of midwives	111
Primary care: delivering the future	39
Primary care: the future	38
Project 2000: a new preparation for practice	71
Promoting better health	34
Protecting children, supporting parents	103
Protection of Children Act 1999	104
Public health: House of Commons Health Committee 2nd report	52
Public health in England	50
Public Interest Disclosure Act 1998	58
Pulling together: the future roles and training of mental health staff	118
Quality strategy for social care	61
Reference guide to consent for examination or treatment	63
Reforming the Mental Health Act	124
The regulation of nurses, midwives and health visitors (JM Consulting)	23
The removal, retention and use of human organs and tissue from post mortem examination	65
Report of the CMO's project to strengthen the public health function	53
Report of the post registration education and practice project	71

title	page
Report of the proposals for the future of community education and practice	36
Report of the public inquiry into children's heart surgery: learning from Bristol (Kennedy report)	64
Report of the taskforce on the strategy for research in nursing (Webb report)	18
Report on the review of patient identifiable information (the Caldicott report)	56
Review of prescribing, supply and administration of medicines (Crown report)	25
The rights of the child: a guide to the UN convention	93
The Roy report	36
RCN mental health nursing strategy	120
Safeguarding standards	55
Safer services (Appleby report)	121
Saving lives: our healthier nation	51
Second report: public health: House of Commons Health Committee	52
Seen but not heard	95
Setting standards for adolescents in hospital	92
Setting standards for children in health care (NAWCH quality review)	91
Setting standards for children undergoing surgery	94
Shaping the future NHS: long-term planning for hospitals and related services	28
Shifting the balance of power: securing delivery	30
Signposts for success	129
Skill mix in primary care	48
Small fortunes	102
Social inequalities 2000	47
The specific health needs of children and young people: Health Committee 2nd report	98
The spectrum of care: local services for people with mental health problems	116
Standards for specialist education and practice	74

title	page
The standards we expect	56
Strategies for living	124
A strategy for nursing	17
Supporting doctors, protecting patients	60
The Sutherland report	85
Tackling drugs to build a better Britain	119
Tackling obesity	52
Targeting practice	49
That bit of help	84
Through a glass darkly: community care and elderly people	81
Tomorrow's nurses and midwives	75
Valuing people	130
Vision 2000	113
A vision for the future	19
Voices in partnership	119
Voices, values and health	66

title	page
The way to go home	87
The Webb report	18
Welfare of children and young people in hospital	92
The Winterton report	109
Witholding or withdrawing life saving treatment (McIntosh report)	97
With respect to old age: long term care - rights and responsibilities (Sutherland report)	85
Working for patients	17
Working for patients: working paper 10	71
Working in partnership: a collaborative approach to care (Butterworth report)	115
Working together, learning together	78
Working together to safeguard children	103
Your guide to the NHS	62
Youth matters	102

the contributors:

Anne Brown

Subject Librarian: Health Studies, University of Plymouth,
The Library, Cornwall College, Trevenson Road, Pool, Nr REDRUTH, Cornwall TR15 3RD
☎ 01209 616183
fax: 01209 616184
email: anneb@cornwall.ac.uk

Lyn Crecy*

Subject Librarian: Health Studies, University of Plymouth,
Learning Resources Centre, Somerset College of Arts and Technology,
Wellington Road, TAUNTON TA1 5AX, Somerset
☎ 01823 366389
fax: 01823 366411
email: lcrecy@plymouth.ac.uk

Anne Henderson

Subject Librarian: Health Studies, University of Plymouth,
The Library, University of Plymouth, Earl Richards Road, EXETER EX2 6AS
☎ 01392 475056
fax: 01392 475053
email: alhenderson@plymouth.ac.uk

Susan Martin

Trust Librarian, South Devon Healthcare NHS Trust
Trust Library, Torbay Hospital, Lawes Bridge, TORQUAY TQ2 7AA
☎ 01803 654704
fax: 01803 616395
email: Susan.Martin@sdevonhc-tr.swest.nhs.uk

Nicola Tricker

Subject Librarian: Health Studies, University of Plymouth,
The Library, University of Plymouth, Drake Circus, PLYMOUTH PL4 8AA
☎ 01752 232308
email: ntricker@plymouth.ac.uk

* for editorial enquiries contact **Lyn Crecy**